Practical Work in Secondary Science

Also available from Continuum

Getting the Buggers into Science, Christine Farmery

Reflective Teaching of Science 11–18, John Parkinson

Teaching and Learning Science, Judith Bennett

Teaching Science 3–11, Christine Farmery

Practical Work in Secondary Science

A Minds-On Approach

Ian Abrahams

continuum

Continuum International Publishing Group

The Tower Building	80 Maiden Lane
11 York Road	Suite 704
London SE1 7NX	New York, NY 10038

www.continuumbooks.com

British Library Cataloguing-in-Publication Data
A catalogue record for this book is available from the British Library.

ISBN: 978-1-8470-6503-2 (hardcover)
          978-1-8470-6504-9 (paperback)

Library of Congress Cataloging-in-Publication Data
Abrahams, Ian.
Practical work in secondary science : a minds-on approach /
Ian Abrahams.
      p. cm.
Includes bibliographical references and index.
ISBN 978-1-84706-503-2 (hardback) – ISBN 978-1-84706-504-9 (pbk.)
1. Science–Study and teaching (Secondary)–United States.
2. Inquiry-based learning–United States. 3. Educational technology–
Study and teaching (Secondary)–United States. I. Title.

Q183.3.A1A222 2010
507.1'273–dc22

2010002902

Typeset by Newgen Imaging Systems Pvt Ltd, Chennai, India
Printed and bound in India by Replika Press Pvt Ltd

Contents

Acknowledgements

In the words of John Donne (1624) "No man is an island" and, in writing this book, I am no exception. Indeed I am immensely grateful to all those schools, teachers and pupils who welcomed me into their lessons and, most importantly, shared with me their thoughts and ideas about practical work. While their anonymity, as part of a research study, prevents me from naming them I hope, if they read this book, they will recognize themselves and accept my sincere thanks for all their help and enthusiasm. Likewise, while the ideas in this book are my own, I have benefited immensely from having been able to discuss them with academics, teachers and many of my students. While I cannot possibly name all of those concerned I would particularly like to take this opportunity to express my thanks to Robin Millar, Ralph Levinson, Fred Lubben, Murat Saglam, Rachael Sharpe, Gill Knights and Mary Chapman whose constructive criticisms have, over the years, helped me to clarify and refine my ideas in the area of practical work. Finally, I would like to thank my wife, Karen, and our children Amos, Aya and Arik for allowing me to spend so much time writing and it is therefore with great pleasure that I dedicate this book to them.

Introduction

Preamble

One of the features of science education that sets it apart from most other subjects taught in school, perhaps *the* distinctive feature, is that it involves practical lessons. Throughout this book I will use the term 'practical work', rather than 'laboratory work' or 'experiments', to describe the kind of lesson activity in which the pupils are involved in manipulating and/or observing real (as opposed to virtual) objects and materials. This is because an 'experiment', particularly in philosophy of science, is generally taken to mean a planned intervention in the material world to test a prediction derived from a theory or hypothesis. Many school science practical tasks, however, do not have this form. And while many practical lessons are undertaken in specifically designed and purpose-built laboratories (White, 1988), the type of activity I want to consider is characterized by the kinds of things students do, rather than where they do them. Yet, having made this distinction, it is worth noting that most practical work in school science does take place in the laboratory (Millar, 1987b), so most school 'practical work' is, in fact, 'laboratory work'. Indeed the House of Commons Science and Technology Committee (2002), when discussing resources for practical work, make no reference to any practical work other than that undertaken in the laboratory.

Practical work is, from my own experience as a physics teacher, not only widely, but also frequently, used in the teaching of science in English secondary schools. One possible reason for this, as Donnelly (1998) has suggested, is that many science teachers see the frequent use of practical work as an essential part of what it *means* to be 'a science teacher'. That practical work 'seems the "natural" and "right" thing to do' (Millar, 2002 p. 53) means that many teachers see its use as the basic modus operandi for the teaching of science. The risk that this presents is that the use of practical work can become so routine that teachers cease to assess critically whether it is always the most appropriate way of achieving a specific learning outcome.

My own interest in practical work was kindled when a head of department challenged my decision to demonstrate current and voltage in parallel circuits using a teacher demonstration, rather than allowing the pupils to carry out the practical task for themselves. While the precise details of the discussion between us have long since been forgotten, the general thrust of his argument was that for pupils to learn it was essential for them to be allowed to do and discover it for themselves. He was a highly experienced teacher, I a new entrant to the profession, and so for a number of years I taught parallel circuits through the use of a class practical. Despite my pupils appearing to enjoy practical work I became increasingly concerned about the effectiveness of practical work as a means of developing conceptual understanding. This concern arose from the fact that in practical lessons most of my time (as well as that of my pupils) was devoted to procedural issues such as collecting, setting up and successfully operating equipment in order to generate the desired data and/or phenomena, to such an extent that conceptual development was either marginalized or, in some cases, squeezed out of the lesson altogether.

But the effectiveness of practical work was not my only concern. Despite the fact that I, and my colleagues in the science department, saw practical work as a source of pupil motivation – a view supported, for example, by Ben-Zvi et al. (1977), Henry (1975) and Jakeways (1986) – and therefore used it as often as possible, the number of our pupils choosing to study science in the post-compulsory phase of their education was at best static (biology) and at worst steadily declining (physics and chemistry). That this was in no sense a situation unique to the school in which I was teaching can be seen from the fact that although there is a frequent and widespread use of practical work in English schools (Bennett, 2003; Millar, 2004; TIMSS, 1999) the absolute number of pupils choosing to pursue science at 'A' level has been in steady decline (Osborne et al., 2003). This decline, so the House of Commons Science and Technology

Committee (2002) reports, is most pronounced in chemistry and physics: the two science subjects that, in my experience, offer the most practical work during Key Stages 3 and 4.

My interest aroused, I undertook an MA in Education. However, rather than resolving my concerns about the effectiveness and affective value of practical work, that study illustrated to me, through the disparate views expressed within the educational literature, the extent to which these issues had not yet been resolved. Moreover, while some literature was informed by research there was 'a large amount of literature which can best be characterized as opinion-based rather than research-based. Tied to these opinions or assumptions are the goals and objectives science educators consider desirable for science teaching and learning' (Blosser, 1981 p. 7). The only firm conclusion that I was able to reach was that there was little useful research-based information on the general effectiveness and affective value of practical work that could be used to help teachers within the context of their own teaching practice.

A number of years later, when provided with the opportunity to undertake a full-time doctorate in education, I decided to look, in greater depth, at the issue of the effectiveness and affective value of practical work. While the findings of that study were written up as a thesis (Abrahams, 2005) that, in turn, lead to a number of academic articles (Abrahams, 2009; Abrahams, 2007a and b; Abrahams and Millar, 2008) I am conscious, having been a teacher myself, as well as having worked on various Initial Teacher Training programmes, that in order to be of use to both teachers and trainee teachers these findings need to be presented in a widely accessible book.

The purpose of this book

Langeveld (1965) has made clear that

> [e]ducational studies . . . are a 'practical science' in the sense that we do not only want to know facts and to understand relations for the sake of knowledge, we want to know and understand in order to be able to act and act 'better' than we did before. (p. 4)

The purpose of this book is therefore to present a piece of academic educational research, that would not have been accessible to the vast majority of teachers, in a more readily accessible format so that teachers can use the findings to inform, and hopefully further develop, their own practice. The style of the book – a combination of a text book, School Science Review article and thesis – aims to combine 'readability' with academic content (although the reader who wishes to probe some of these issues in greater depth – possibly as part of a Master's level course – is advised to refer to the original thesis and/or articles cited). Rather than continually referencing the study that I undertook the reader is advised that all of the data used within this book is drawn from a three year study (Abrahams, 2005) and that as you read through this book I hope that some of the 'flavour' of that original study comes through.

That said, my primary aim is not to convince you of the validity of my findings – although it is certainly part of what I hope to do – but rather to cause you to think about *why* you believe that *how* **you** use practical work is effective and has affective value and the *evidence* that you have to support this.

To avoid focusing on the effectiveness and affective value of one or two potentially atypical pieces of practical work this book draws on examples of practical work used in 25 biology, chemistry and physics lessons in the teaching of a wide range of topics, to pupils of various ages and academic abilities. While 25 lessons is still clearly a relatively small sample of the range of possible practical work it is of sufficient size to illustrate the generic issues relating to the effectiveness and affective value of practical work that are at the heart of this book.

The book has two broad themes. The first relates to the general effectiveness of practical work as used in biology, chemistry and physics lessons across the compulsory phase of secondary education (Key Stages 3 and 4). This is because, as a science teacher, it seems both reasonable and highly relevant to ask (and want to know the answer to) whether, given its disproportionately high cost and the relatively large proportion of the teaching time that it occupies, practical work is an effective use of both teaching time and available resources. The second theme relates to the issue of whether practical work has an affective value (in addition to any cognitive value) and, if so, in what sense this manifests itself. From a science teacher's perspective there is, I would argue, one extremely relevant measure of the affective value of practical work and that is whether pupils choose to pursue science beyond the end of Key Stage 4 and, if so, which of the sciences they prefer to study and why.

The structure of the educational system in English schools

While the issues covered in this book are relevant for all science teachers who use practical work within their teaching, the research upon which the book is based was carried out in state maintained comprehensive schools in England and it may therefore be useful, before proceeding further, to briefly describe the structure of the educational system in English schools.

All pupils in English state maintained schools are required to follow a National Curriculum for the 11 years of their compulsory education with these being divided up into four, unequally spaced, Key Stages a term that is peculiar to the United Kingdom. Education in primary and junior school corresponds to Key Stages 1 and 2 respectively (Years 1–6 which corresponds to ages 5–11). Key Stage 3 covers the first three years at secondary school (Years 7, 8 and 9 – ages 11–14) at the end of which pupils select some of the subjects they want to continue to study during the two years (Years 10 and 11 – ages 15–16) that constitute Key Stage 4 that ends with the pupils sitting their public examinations (GCSEs). Although pupils have some choice as to the subjects they study during Key Stage 4 it is a statutory requirement that they continue to study Science, along with English and Mathematics, until the end of Year 11 with all science teaching having been governed by the National Curriculum since 1989. Finally Key Stage 5 corresponds to the two years of post-compulsory secondary school education (pupils aged 17–18) and any students studying science at this stage are doing so by choice rather than compulsion.

In terms of who teaches what science subject the current system in England is one in which science is taught to pupils in Key Stage 3 as a combined subject with the same teacher often teaching all of the various biology, chemistry and physics components to the same pupils. In this respect it can be seen that, on average, non-subject specialists are teaching two-thirds of Key Stage 3 material. While science in Key Stage 4 is designed to be taught as three separate subjects, each of which is taught by a subject specialist, Millar (1987a) has pointed out that shortages – particularly in the number of physics teachers – have inevitably meant that physics lessons in some schools are being taught by teachers who themselves only studied physics up to Key Stage 4.

Overview of the book

Following on from this introduction, Chapter 1 considers the way in which the perceived emphasis as to the purpose[s] of practical work has changed over time. I will put these changes into the context of a number of key historical episodes that have been influential in changing the way in which teachers and policy makers think about the nature and purpose of practical work in the teaching of science. Having discussed these historical changes in emphasis I will then present details of five of the widely accepted purposes in more depth. Chapter 2 considers the affective value of practical work and starts with a discussion of the psychological literature on motivation and interest. It then shows, by reference to the literature and comments made by teachers in the study, that the meaning of the terms 'motivation' and 'interest', at least within many educational contexts, bears little resemblance to their meaning in a strict psychological sense. The chapter then goes on to provide a way of understanding the seemingly contradictory fact that pupils can both claim to like practical work and also express a firm intention to drop science at the end of Key Stage 4. Chapter 3 discusses key issues regarding the effectiveness of practical work and what you can do to maximize the effectiveness of any practical task that you decide to use. In Chapter 4 I consider what pupils learn from doing practical work and why, sometimes, this might not be the same as the teacher intended. Chapter 5 looks at a specific example of how one very experienced teacher used some of the ideas discussed in this book to maximize the effectiveness of their practical lessons. Finally Chapter 6 draws together the ideas of the previous chapters to present an overview of the effectiveness and affective value of practical work and suggests the implications of these ideas in terms of practice.

The Purpose of Practical Work

Introduction

Despite 200 years of debate, and the large amount of literature that has been written on the subject, Millar (1987b) can still reasonably ask

> But what is this practical work for, and what learning does it promote? Its very taken-for-grantedness means that this question is often not asked; we find it hard to imagine school science without a strong practical emphasis. We reply simply that 'science is a practical subject' and leave it at that. (p. 113)

While it is of questionable value to try to define precisely the start of the debate into the purpose and value of practical work it is useful to see that by as early as the end of the eighteenth century Edgeworth and Edgeworth (1811, the first edition appeared in 1798) were already claiming that:

> The great difficulty which has been found in attempts to instruct children in science has, we apprehend, arisen from the theoretic manner in which preceptors have proceeded. The knowledge that cannot be immediately applied to use, has no interest . . . they may learn the principles of mechanics . . . but if they have no means of applying their knowledge, it is quickly forgotten . . . Their senses should

be exercised in experiments, and these experiments should be simple, distinct, and applicable to some object in which our pupils are immediately interested. (p. 723)

While a small number of schools had previously used practical work it was not until 1860 when the Science and Art Department, stimulated by the growing needs of industry, started to provide funding in order to increase the extent and scope of the use of practical work in English schools.

Despite this increase, the main reason for what was still a very limited amount of practical work, which tended to be of the form of teacher demonstration, remained the practical verification of previously taught scientific ideas. Things changed markedly in 1884 when Armstrong proposed the introduction of a 'heuristic', or discovery based, approach to science education. He later wrote, 'Heuristic methods of teaching are methods which involve our placing students as far as possible in the attitude of discovery – methods which involve their *finding out* instead of being merely told about things' (Armstrong, 1903 p. 236. Italics in original).

This conviction, still shared by many teachers today, that pupils need to discover facts about science for themselves led Armstrong to place great store by the physical manipulation of apparatus and the development of what he believed would be transferable psycho-motor skills. Indeed, Armstrong suggests that 'The power of devising and fitting up apparatus, as well as devising and carrying out experiments is cultivated. Thus handiness is acquired' (Armstrong, 1903 p. 257).

With the wide and rapid acceptance of the heuristic approach within the school system the perceived purpose of practical work shifted away from content and towards the provision of an insight into scientific method and the acquisition of relevant skills. Yet things were to change again following the publication of the findings of the highly influential Thomson Report:

We are driven to the conclusion that in many schools more time is spent in laboratory work than the results obtained can justify . . . . Insistence on the view that experiments by the class must always be preferred to demonstration experiments leads to great waste of time and provides an inferior substitute. (Thomson, 1918 pp. 21–2)

The result of its publication was to be the demise of the heuristic approach in school science and its replacement by one in which the main purpose of practical work was seen as being the development of conceptual understanding. Practical work was, from this perspective, to be considered justifiable only in so far as it offered support to the learning process. There was no longer seen to be any justification for practical work per se since the purpose of its use had switched to the support that it offered pupils in terms of providing reinforcement of conceptual knowledge taught using other methods.

After the publication of the Norwood Report (1943), in which a curtailed programme of practical work was advocated, the justification for its use shifted back once again to that of enabling pupils to acquire physical skills that would be transferable to future employment in the rapidly expanding technological industries. By the 1950s the arguments that had been raised against a heuristic approach by the Thomson Report (1918) had all but been forgotten. In fact the influential Report of the Science Masters' Association (1953) stated, quite unequivocally, that pressure on teaching time could best be overcome, not by a reduction in individual investigation and a more judicious use of teacher demonstration, but by the narrowing of the syllabus. Furthermore, they proposed that

> As much experimental work as possible should be done individually or in groups – in fact, the whole of the science course can well be built around experiments which children perform. There is so much material to be taught that any part of the syllabus that does not lend itself to individual work might well be omitted. (p. 5)

The change in emphasis that accompanied the resurgence of the heuristic approach, coupled with pioneering work by Bruner (1961), gave rise in Britain to the development of the Nuffield discovery based learning courses. By the late 1960s the Nuffield view of 'the pupil as scientist' who needed to *do* science in order to *understand* science; a position encapsulated in the much quoted proverb that 'I hear and I forget, I see and I remember, I do and I understand', was firmly established.

Yet by the late 1970s and early 1980s there were mounting doubts about the claim that 'doing' leads to 'understanding' (Driver, 1983; Hodson, 1992; Tasker, 1981). In addition, there was a growing realization that the conceptual demands that were required for discovery learning to be successful were beyond the ability of the overwhelming majority of academically average pupils (Bates, 1978; Bennett, 2003; Lazarowitz and Tamir, 1994). Concern was also expressed (Kreitler and Kreitler, 1974) that in some courses, such as Nuffield Combined Science, the shift away from the transfer of conceptual knowledge had gone too far and had spawned approaches that were almost devoid of conceptual content. At the same time Shulman and Tamir (1973) suggested that this change in emphasis meant, ipso facto, that the laboratory *itself* had become the very essence of the science learning process. The growing doubts regarding the discovery learning approach were succinctly summarized by Driver's (1983) oft-cited counter-claim of 'I do and I am even more confused' (p. 9).

During the 1980s criticism of discovery learning led to the emergence of an alternative approach to practical work that had evolved out of an earlier American scheme, *Science – A Process Approach (SAPA)* (American Association for the Advancement of Science (AAAS), 1967). This approach, exemplified in England by the *Warwick Process Science* (Screen, 1986), was dominated by an emphasis on the processes of science, as epitomized by practising scientists, with little emphasis on scientific facts or concepts. Commenting on this lack of emphasis on scientific facts Screen (1986) suggested that 'the most valuable aspects of a scientific education are those that remain after the facts have been forgotten' (Quoted in Bennett, 2003 p. 89).

This shift in emphasis towards the processes of science was also reflected in the way educational courses and materials were, by the late 1980s, keen to be seen to associate themselves with the process-led approach (Millar, 1989b). Indeed the dominance of the process-led approach was affirmed in a Department of Education and Science Policy Statement (DES 1985) that stressed that *the* essential characteristic of education in science was the introduction of pupils to the *methods* of science.

Yet by the late 1980s and early 1990s there was a growing chorus of criticism of this approach (Hodson, 1992; Millar, 1989b; Millar and Driver, 1987; Wellington, 1989). In particular it was argued (Millar, 1989b; Millar and Driver, 1987) that content independent processes, such as classifying, hypothesizing, lateral thinking and observing, could not be taught; they are simply *abilities* that all individuals have a natural propensity to develop and that are evident even in children of a very young age. This was not the only perceived problem with the process approach which also came in for criticism on the grounds that 'In recent years there has been a tendency, in some quarters, to give such priority to the processes of science that content has come to be regarded as relatively unimportant' (Hodson, 1992 p. 68). The pendulum had swung back the other way yet again.

Five suggested purposes for the use of practical work

Although the perceived importance of one particular purpose for using practical work has, as we have seen, risen (and subsequently fallen) at the expense of another, the number of suggested purposes, upon which there is general consensus, is relatively small. In this section I want to consider each of the five purposes for its use that have been suggested by Hodson (1990), these being:

1. To enhance the learning of scientific knowledge.
2. To teach laboratory skills.
3. To develop certain 'scientific attitudes' such as open-mindedness, objectivity and willingness to suspend judgement.
4. To give insight into scientific method, and develop expertise in using it.
5. To motivate pupils, by stimulating interest and enjoyment.

While I will deal with all five points the last point, which deals with the affective value of practical work rather than its effective value, will be dealt with in greater depth, in Chapter 2.

To enhance the learning of scientific knowledge

One of the reasons that teachers and pupils alike give for wanting to do practical work is that they believe, as the following examples illustrate, that it enhances the learning of scientific knowledge.

> Mrs Kettlesing: I think they learn so much more by actually doing it than by just being told or even watching me do it.
> Pupil DE17: If you do it yourself as a practical instead of from a book it makes it easier to learn what you need to know for the exam.

Yet despite such claims research findings into the effectiveness of practical work as a means of enhancing the development of conceptual understanding remain ambiguous. Hewson and Hewson (1983) report a significant enhancement of pupils' conceptual understanding among that half of their study group, of pupils aged 13–20, who had received a primarily practical-based instruction compared to the other half of the study group that had received a traditional non-practical instruction. However, in other similar studies such findings have not been duplicated. Indeed Mulopo and Fowler (1987), in a study of 120 Grade 11 pupils studying chemistry, reported no significant difference in the level of conceptual understanding among pupils irrespective of whether they had been taught using either practical or traditional non-practical methods. In contrast they report that the most appreciable factor in determining the extent of conceptual development was not the method of instruction but rather the pupil's level of intellectual development.

Major reviews of the literature, within both the first and second editions of the *Handbook of Research on Teaching* (Shulman and Tamir, 1973; Watson, 1963), and subsequent reviews relating specifically to practical work (Bates, 1978; Blosser, 1981; Hofstein and Lunetta, 1982; Lazarowitz and Tamir, 1994) have all concluded, when outcomes are measured using pen and paper tests, that the use of practical work offers no significant advantage in the development of pupils' scientific conceptual understanding.

Although Hofstein and Lunetta (1982) note that as with a glass that can optimistically be said to be half full and pessimistically half empty, the same is true regarding the effectiveness of practical work in so far as 'Many of these studies have reported nonsignificant results, meaning that the laboratory medium was *at least* as effective in promoting student growth on the variable measured as were more conventional modes of instruction' (p. 212. Italics added). However, given the central role of the laboratory in the new curriculum, its high financial cost and the high aspirations that accompanied its introduction, these non-significant findings, corroborated by further recent studies (Burron et al., 1993; Chang and Lederman, 1994; Jackman and Moellenberg, 1987; Watson et al., 1995), led Clackson and Wright (1992) to summarize the situation thus:

> Although practical work is commonly considered to be invaluable in science teaching, research shows that it is not necessarily so valuable in science *learning*. The evidence points to the uncomfortable conclusion that much laboratory work has been of little benefit in helping pupils and students understand concepts. (p. 40)

Furthermore, Yager et al. (1969) argue that some academically able pupils in fact consider laboratory work to be a waste of their time, serving only to delay their pursuit of new theories and concepts. In response Connell (1971) suggests that even *if* this were the case, a point he argues requires further investigation to establish, it would more than likely only be indicative of a mismatch between the practical work and the pupils' academic ability. Similarly van den Berg and Giddings (1992) argue that such beliefs, if held by the pupils, would be a criticism of the form of specific practical tasks rather than constituting a criticism of practical work per se.

Indeed many of these arguments seem, generally speaking, to reinforce Ausubel's (1968) assertion that 'In dividing the labour of scientific instruction, the laboratory typically carries the burden of conveying the method and the spirit of science whereas the textbook and teachers assume the burden of transmitting subject matter and content' (p. 346). It is important to note that Ausubel goes on to make a distinction in this context between different forms of laboratory work and states that 'Laboratory work in this context refers to inductive or hypothetico-deductive discovery experiences and should not be confused with [teacher] demonstrations' (p. 346). However, Millar (1998) has questioned whether the observation of specific phenomena within the context of a practical task can, unaided, lead to the development of conceptual understanding. In this context it has been proposed (Brodin, 1978; Millar et al., 1999) that the function of practical work might be better understood in terms of a link, or bridge, between *previously* taught scientific concepts and subsequent observations.

One explanation that has been advanced (Tamir, 1991) for the lack of research evidence to support the use of practical work as an effective means for developing pupils' conceptual knowledge is that, in contrast to teacher demonstration, its use can generate cognitive overload. Cognitive overload occurs as a consequence of simultaneous demands being made of the pupils by practical work that requires them to apply intellectual and practical skills as well as prior knowledge (Johnstone and Wham, 1982).

Therefore, despite the frequent claims that one purpose of practical work is to provide an effective means of developing conceptual understanding, research findings suggest, at least when the outcomes are measured using pen and paper tests (and you might like to consider whether this approach is justified), that there is no significant advantage (or disadvantage) to its use.

To teach laboratory skills

One of the difficulties in considering the effectiveness of practical work in the teaching of laboratory skills is that the term 'skill' has been used to mean different things by different people in different studies (Bennett, 2003). Hofstein and Lunetta (1982) argue that many studies take too narrow a view of laboratory skills and consequently neglect to measure development in skill areas such as creative thinking, problem solving, general intellectual development, observing and classifying. Hodson (1990) distinguishes between 'craft skills' which are content specific – for example learning to read a micrometer or carrying out a titration – and content independent skills such as observation and manual dexterity which are generalizable to other contexts or disciplines. Although, it is interesting to note that Gott and Duggan (1995) question the appropriateness of even using the term 'skill' to describe *any* content independent processes. Dawe (2003) argues that content independent skills are, because of their generalizability, of more value to *all* pupils while content specific skills are of value primarily to future scientists or technicians. However, Ausubel (1968) argues, with regard to problem-solving skills, that there is no reason to believe that even *if* they could be taught, in the context of one subject, that they could be transferred to other contexts or disciplines. While Heaney (1971) reports that a heuristic approach leads to the development of problem-solving skills and that a more traditional 'didactic-with-demonstration' approach is actually detrimental to the development of such skills this finding has not been confirmed in any other study. Indeed it has been argued (Millar, 1989a; Millar and Driver, 1987) that content independent processes cannot in fact be taught but are, rather, innate abilities that we all have a natural propensity to develop. Similarly studies into pupils' perspectives about laboratory work (Boud et al., 1980; Osborne, 1976) report that pupils themselves do not believe that their problem-solving skills improve as a consequence of undertaking practical work.

Similar ambiguity surrounds the effectiveness of practical work in the development of creative thinking. Hill (1976), using the Minnesota Test of Creative Thinking, reported an improvement in creativity after pupil involvement in practical work in chemistry. In contrast Gangoli and Gurumurthy (1995), using an 'objective-type' test devised and standardized by Gurumurthy (1988), reported no evidence of improvement in creative thinking within their study.

Hofstein (1988) has pointed out that if the term 'skill' is interpreted narrowly to mean only 'manipulative skill' then practical work has, perhaps unsurprisingly, been found to have a measurable advantage over other non-practical types of instruction within science education (Ben-Zvi et al., 1977; Gangoli and Gurumurthy, 1995; Kempa and Palmer, 1974). However, while not denying its relative effectiveness in this area White (1996, 1979) and Clackson and Wright (1992) have questioned both the appropriateness, and cost effectiveness, of its use as a means for developing content independent manual dexterity with White (1979) suggesting that 'if skill in manipulation *per se* is the aim, not merely skill with scientific apparatus, there are cheaper and probably more efficient and effective ways of developing it. Needlework and fine woodwork are instances' (p. 762). Such criticism echoes that made about sixty years earlier in the British Association Report (1917) in which it was suggested that some purposes for undertaking laboratory work are of an intrinsically lesser value than others and that 'In the laboratory the development of dexterity and skill is only a secondary consideration' (British Association Report, 1917. Quoted in Connell, 1971 p. 138).

Responding to the almost total ambiguity of research findings regarding the value of laboratory work, Hofstein and Lunetta (1982) claim that: (i) similarly ambiguous results have been found when studying *any* attempt to improve teaching and that, (ii) many past studies contained design weaknesses that render the conclusions drawn problematic.

To develop certain 'scientific attitudes' such as open-mindedness, objectivity and willingness to suspend judgement

The term 'scientific attitude' is both broad and weakly defined. Indeed it has been pointed out (Gardner, 1975) that the term 'attitude' has been appropriated by different researchers to describe on the one hand 'scientific attitudes' and on the other hand 'attitudes towards science'. Aiken and Aiken (1969) discussing traits such as intellectual honesty, open mindedness and curiosity referred to them as 'the more cognitive scientific attitudes' (p. 295). In contrast, Hofstein and Lunetta (1982) use the term 'attitude' when discussing the development of 'favourable attitudes toward science' (p. 210). There has been relatively little research (Hofstein and Lunetta, 1982) to evaluate the effectiveness of practical work as a means of developing scientific attitudes although in marked contrast it has been pointed out (Simon, 2000) that there have been in excess of two hundred studies into attitudes towards science.

Part of the explanation for this is to be found in terms of differences between the generic aims for practical work used by different researchers. Thus while Shulman and Tamir (1973) place both attitude and interest towards science in the same generic category, Hodson (1990), whose categories I am using in this book, places them into different generic categories and, as such, the term 'attitude' relates only to scientific attitudes and not to attitudes towards science.

Yet even when the term 'attitude' is used only with regard to scientific attitudes there is little evidence within the literature as to what constitutes a scientific attitude or, more importantly, how these are determined. Thus while Henry (1975) suggests that scientific attitudes include the need: (i) to be observant, (ii) careful, (iii) patient and (iv) persistent, Lazarowitz and Tamir (1994) suggest a much expanded list of scientific attitudes that includes 'honesty, readiness to admit failure, critical assessment of the results and their limitations, curiosity, risk taking, objectivity, precision, confidence, perseverance, responsibility, collaboration, and readiness to reach consensus' (p. 98).

However, from a study of 17 senior biology laboratories Fordham (1980) reported that the pursuit of scientifically correct results meant that honesty, far from being a scientific attitude that was developed through the use of practical work, was frequently its first casualty in so far as

> If the experiment doesn't work we go to somebody else and get their results . . . it looks better when you get the results that you are supposed to . . . it's pretty obvious you won't get as good a mark as someone who got it to work. (p. 114)

Despite differences as to what might, or might not, be considered an appropriate scientific attitude Gauld and Hukins (1980) have pointed out that the majority of the scientific attitudes that appear in the literature fall into three generic categories: (i) general attitudes towards scientific ideas, (ii) attitudes towards the evaluation of scientific ideas and (iii) commitment to a particular set of beliefs about science. From a more fundamental perspective Bennett (2003) has argued that despite the difference between scientific attitudes and attitudes towards science, both are inextricably linked with behaviours, dispositions and beliefs rendering a clear-cut distinction between them highly problematic.

In conclusion Gardner and Gould (1990) claim, with regard to the development of scientific attitudes, that 'While students generally enjoy hands-on experience and the opportunity to work individually or in small groups, we cannot conclude that such experiences will, by themselves, bring about major changes in styles of thinking' (p. 151).

To give insight into scientific method and develop expertise in using it

Lazarowitz and Tamir (1994) have claimed that it is by undertaking practical work that pupils will develop an understanding of the nature of science, the way scientists work and in particular 'the multiplicity of scientific methods' (p. 98). Yet such a multiplicity of methods is often overlooked given the strength of the prevailing view of the scientific enterprise (Bennett, 2003) that is firmly embedded within a hypothetico-deductive (Popper, 1989) view of science. In this context Bencze (1996) has argued that undue emphasis on a hypothetico-deductive view of science has, as a consequence, meant that science education has failed to reflect the fact that much of the research reported within the media is based on correlational studies that involve blind testing – methods that are rarely used within school laboratories. Millar (1989a) has pointed out that even if the hypothetico-deductive view of science *is* an appropriate model for the scientific enterprise it does not accurately represent the nature of practical work as it occurs within the school laboratory.

Indeed Martin (1979) has claimed that much practical work undertaken within the school laboratory has been reflective of 'dubious or discarded philosophies of science' (p.331), a reference to the now widely discredited inductive view of science (Millar, 2004) that underpins discovery learning. In the same context Layton (1990) has questioned the extent to which any philosophy of science has been used to systematically guide the nature of practical work in the school laboratory noting that 'the philosophy of science has rarely been used in a systematic and deliberate manner as a prime source of objectives for student laboratory work' (p. 37).

Hodson (1989) has argued that the perceptions about both the nature of science and scientific method are shaped by the distorted manner in which text-books portray the relationship between experiment and theory in that 'The actual chronology of experiment and theory is rewritten in text-books. This helps to sustain the myth that the path of science is certain and assigns a simple clear cut role to experiments' (p. 57).

Matthews and Winchester (1989) suggest that only if pupils are allowed to see that science is often less than certain and that the relationship between experiment and theory is not always clear cut will they develop an understanding of scientific method. Lazarowitz and Tamir (1994) suggest that such an approach will mean that 'the distorted image many students have of scientists (unusual persons wearing white gowns, working in isolation, and exhibiting extraordinary behaviour) may be discarded, and students may realize that scientists are ordinary persons' (p. 109).

The role of practical work in motivating pupils

Perhaps the most disappointing fact is that *despite* claims that pupils are said to prefer a laboratory centred approach (Ben-Zvi et al., 1976; Hofstein et al., 1976; Lazarowitz and Tamir, 1994; Pickering, 1987;) and that its use encourages and motivates pupils to study science (Arce and Betancourt, 1997; Ben-Zvi et al., 1976; Hannon, 1994; Kerr, 1964; Lazarowitz and Tamir, 1994) there is a broadly shared view (House of Commons Science and Technology Committee, 2002; Jenkins, 1994; Millar and Osborne, 1998; Osborne and Collins, 2001; Osborne et al., 2003; Osborne et al., 1998) that far too many 'young people are, at age 16, closing off the option of entering a career in science or engineering at a time when the United Kingdom is suffering from a shortage of scientists and engineers'. (House of Commons Science and Technology Committee, 2002 p. 23). In fact this is happening *despite* the devotion of a significant proportion of science teaching time to the pursuit of practical work. Indeed Bennett (2003) has argued that there is little reason to believe that the amount of time spent on practical work will have changed appreciably since the studies by Thompson (1975) and Beatty and Woolnough (1982) in which it was found that one-third of all the time allocated to science education, during 'A' level study, is devoted to some form of practical work (Thompson, 1975) with this rising to one half of science teaching time for pupils within the 11–13 age range (Beatty and Woolnough, 1982). In fact the Minister of State for School Standards, (House of Commons Select Committee on Science and Technology,

2002) stated that in terms of the proportion of practical work within science education in the United Kingdom 'The evidence we have . . . the TIMSS assessment . . . which was published in December 2000, indicated that the amount of practical being taken on in schools here is actually greater than is the case elsewhere' (Question number 514).

A recent study by Windschitle and Andre (1998) into pupil motivation and the influence of epistemological beliefs on learning found that practical work was primarily effective in motivating epistemologically more mature pupils and that in contrast the epistemologically less mature pupils found traditional teaching styles more motivating. Other studies (Arce and Betancourt, 1997; Ben-Zvi et al., 1977; Berry et al., 1999; Watson and Fairbrother, 1993) report that pupils are more frequently motivated by practical work in which they are allowed to exercise some degree of control over the design and which they find both challenging and rewarding. Although Lazarowitz and Tamir (1994) suggest that the motivational effectiveness of such tasks can be reduced if it is perceived as too difficult. In the following chapter I will consider, in greater depth, the role of practical work in the affective domain.

What has research to say about the purpose of practical work?

Having looked at each of the five purposes of practical work suggested by Hodson (1990) I would suggest that the only unambiguous claim to emerge from the research is that practical work is, undeniably, more effective at developing manual dexterity than other, non-practical, methods of teaching science. However, unless I am very much mistaken, such a claim seems to be saying no more than would the rather unsurprising one that playing the oboe is more effective at developing manual dexterity than not playing a musical instrument! Furthermore, such a claim does not even begin to address the question as to the relative effectiveness of practical work in developing manual dexterity compared with, for example, tying a shoelace, mending a bicycle tyre puncture, playing the oboe or even taking up origami.

Where does all this apparent ambiguity leave you the teacher? I think that part of the answer to this, as Duschl and Gitomer (1997) have suggested, is that science teachers tend to think of their teaching in terms of 'tasks and activities rather than conceptual structures and scientific reasoning' (p. 65). If this is in fact the case (and you might think about the extent to which this approach describes your own teaching practice) then science teachers do not consciously think about their use of practical work in terms of a specific purpose (or even a combination of purposes). Instead, as Donnelly (1998) suggests, they use it because they believe unquestioningly that to do so is an essential part of 'being a good science teacher'. In this respect when such teachers are asked to justify their use of a specific practical task they typically respond (Abrahams, 2005) with one, or more, of the purposes suggested by Hodson (1990) because those are the responses that they believe 'being a good science teacher' requires that they give when asked such a question. Such responses, I would argue, tell us more about the rhetoric of practical work, about the prevailing view as to the purpose of practical work at a particular point in time, than about the actual practice itself.

The important point here though is not to focus too much on any specific purpose of practical work but rather to consider why so many teachers, despite any clear research evidence, are apparently so willing to accept the prevailing rhetoric in such an unquestioning manner. The lack of any unambiguous evidence reinforces the point made by Bates (1978) over forty years ago that:

> Teachers who believe that the laboratory accomplishes something special for their students would do well to consider carefully what those outcomes might be, and then to find a way to measure them for the answer has not yet been conclusively found: What does the laboratory accomplish that could not be accomplished as well by less expensive and less time consuming alternatives? (1978 p. 75)

Having considered the purpose of practical work from a theoretical perspective I want to briefly consider what research has shown us about the views that teachers have on the purpose of practical work.

The purpose of practical work: Large-scale national surveys of teachers' views

Surprisingly there have been only four (Abrahams and Saglam, 2010; Beatty, 1980; Kerr, 1964; Thompson, 1975) published research studies into teachers' views on the purpose of practical work. The first of these (Kerr, 1964) asked a sample of secondary school teachers in England to rank ten suggested aims (purposes) for practical work (Table 1.1) in order of their perceived importance.

A similar approach was used by Thompson (1975) although this focused solely on teachers' attitudes to practical work at Key Stage 5 (age 17–18) while

Table 1.1 The ten aims (purposes) of practical work (adapted from Kerr 1964 p. 27)

	Aims of practical work
1	To encourage accurate observation and careful recording
2	To promote simple, common sense, scientific methods of thought
3	To develop manipulative skills
4	To give training in problem-solving
5	To prepare pupils for assessed practical work
6	To elucidate the theoretical work so as to aid comprehension
7	To verify facts and principles already taught
8	To be an integral part of the process of finding facts by investigation and arriving at principles
9	To arouse and maintain interest in the subject
10	To make biological, chemical and physical phenomena more real through actual experience

another (Beatty, 1980) considered attitudes to practical work only among teachers at Key Stage 3 (age 11–14). Although a direct comparison is not possible as the studies by Beatty (1980) and Thompson (1975) both used an expanded list of 20 aims a cautious comparison between can be made by comparing the order of importance of those 10 aims, proposed by Kerr (1964), that are common to all three studies. Bennett (2003) has suggested that despite a certain degree of variation between the studies in terms of teachers, subjects and pupil ages, there was a general consensus that most teachers saw 'most important aims of practical work as being:

- to encourage accurate observation and description;
- to make scientific phenomena more real;
- to enhance understanding of scientific ideas;
- to arouse and maintain interest (particularly in younger pupils);
- to promote a scientific method of thought.' (Bennett, 2003 pp. 78–9)

One point that it is worth noting here, and one I will return to in Chapter 6, is that both Kerr (1964, pp. 43–6) and Thompson (1975, p. 36) report finding marked differences between what teachers say are their aims for doing practical work and the reality of their practice. Interestingly differences have also been reported (Wilkinson and Ward, 1997) between the stated aims Australian teachers gave for using practical work and the aims that their pupils associated with those same practical tasks.

In an interesting comparative study Swain et al. (1999) compared the views of teachers in Egypt, Korea and the United Kingdom and suggested that inter-country differences might be due to differences in curriculum emphasis and/or the nature of the dominant epistemological perspective. In a recent study that I undertook (Abrahams and Saglam, 2010) I used the same 10 aims that had been used by Kerr (1964) to examine whether there had been any changes over time in the views of UK teachers regarding the purpose of practical work. We found that the most substantial change in teachers' aims for practical work occurred at Key Stage 4 (ages 15–16) and it would appear to reflect the introduction of the Sc1 investigations (a practically assessed component of a public examination) and the associated pressure on biology, chemistry and physics teachers that this has generated in terms of needing to prepare pupils for assessed practical work. Indeed Donnelly et al. (1996), in a detailed study of the 'Scientific Enquiry' component of the English National Curriculum (Attainment target Sc1), found that extended, and more open-ended, investigative practical tasks were, in fact, rarely being used to teach pupils about specific aspects of scientific enquiry might have been, but almost entirely to assess their ability to conduct an empirical enquiry 'scientifically' – something that they would be required to do as part of their public examinations. It would seem, therefore, that an unintended consequence for educational policy makers of the introduction of Attainment Target Sc1 may have been that teachers' views about the use of practical work were influenced by government led changes to the assessment procedures (that generate pressure on teachers) – and that this was particularly pronounced at Key Stage 4 (ages 15–16).

Were there to be a decision by educational policy makers in England to remove Sc1 as a means of assessment – and, as such, the pressure on teachers that was associated with it – I would predict, and this would be an interesting area for future research, that the importance of using practical work 'to prepare pupils for assessed practical work – including Sc1 investigations' would return to a position at, or very close to, the bottom of teachers' aims for using practical work at Key Stage 4 (ages 15–16).

While many science teachers at Key Stages 4 and 5 (ages 15–18) substantially decreased the status of the aims 'to encourage accurate observation and careful recording', 'to promote simple, common-sense, scientific methods of thought' and 'to develop manipulative skills', I do not believe that this necessarily means that they no longer see these as important in an objective sense. Rather, we would claim, that such changes are more likely to reflect the fact that teachers recognize, as a result of pressures in the educational environment, that different aims are more important, *relative* to other aims, at different stages within secondary education if their teaching is to be effective. Indeed it might be expected that if these aims were effectively met, for example, in Key Stage 3 – when their importance is ranked highly – then their *relative* importance at Key Stages 4 and 5 might be expected to drop as has been found in this study.

In the next chapter I will consider current perspectives on the nature and purpose of practical work in the affective domain and, in particular, consider the question of the extent to which we might be justified in thinking that its use motivates pupils towards science in general and school science in particular.

Current Perspectives on the Nature and Purpose of Practical Work in the Affective Domain

2

Chapter Outline

Introduction

When science teachers (and many educators working on ITT programmes) are asked why they believe practical work to be such an important part of science education they frequently refer to its motivational value. Science teachers are not alone in holding this belief as similar beliefs about the motivational value of 'hands-on' work in mathematics have also been expressed by maths teachers (Middleton, 1995). Yet, for example, when two science teachers were asked to explain in more detail what they actually meant when they claimed that practical work had a motivational value they responded:

> Mr Rainton: I think in most instances it's short-term engagement for that particular lesson rather than general motivation towards science. In general I think it's very difficult to motivate kids in Year 10 and 11 into thinking about engaging in science and thinking about science in terms of 'that's a career that I want to follow'.
>
> Miss Sharow: A little bit of practical to motivate them so to speak.
>
> ⇨

Researcher: So the purpose of the practical was to motivate?

Miss Sharow: Yes.

Researcher: When you say motivate is that more of a long-term thing, to encourage them to like science, or is it to engage them in that particular lesson?

Miss Sharow: Probably just in the lesson, probably yes.

Are science teachers, we might then ask, using the term 'motivation' in its strict psychological sense or rather as a 'catch-all' term that embodies elements of interest, enjoyment and engagement?

Bandura (1986) suggests that the terms 'motivate' and 'interest' have been used in the literature, and by teachers (Abrahams, 2005), to mean the same thing, even though 'there is a major difference between a motive, which is an inner drive to action, and an interest, which is a fascination with something' (p. 243). For example Woolnough and Allsop (1985) report that the findings of Kerr (1964) have 'shown how highly teachers rate *motivational* factors' (p. 5. Italics added). Yet Kerr (1964) makes no reference to the issue of motivation or motivational factors, suggesting only that one of the aims of practical work is to 'arouse and maintain *interest*' (Kerr, 1964 p. 21). Similarly Lazarowitz and Tamir (1994), when claiming that practical work motivates pupils, cite, in support of their claim, the findings of Ben-Zvi et al. (1977), Henry (1975) and Selemes et al. (1969) although all three of these studies focused on the issue of pupil *interest* rather than *motivation*. Indeed, of the three sources that they cite it is only in one (Henry, 1975) that the term 'motivation' is actually mentioned, and even then it appears only once in the final paragraph, when Henry, citing no supporting evidence, simply states that 'In addition, psychological reasons can be proposed which relate to the improved motivation of pupils by the inclusion of laboratory exercises in the science program' (p. 73).

Furthermore the frequent claims made about the affective value of practical work, both in the literature and among teachers, make it necessary to consider how terms such as 'motivation', 'interest' and 'engagement' can be effectively operationalized. It is, after all, relatively easy to make sweeping claims about the affective value of practical work. It is quite another to state what such claims actually mean in terms of specific observable consequences.

Motivation

In order to distinguish clearly between 'motivation' and 'interest', I will use the term 'motivation' to refer to anything that engenders 'an inner drive to action'

(Bandura, 1986, p. 243) while the term 'interest' will, following the definition proposed by Krapp et al. (1992), be used to refer 'to a person's interaction with a *specific* class of tasks, objects, events or ideas' (p. 8. Italics in original). Motivation, is therefore an enthusiasm for and/or curiosity about science that, in terms of observable consequences, might manifest itself in your pupils' decision to actively pursue the study of one, or more, science subjects in the post-compulsory phase of their education or in additional voluntary actions that they might undertake. Such actions might include their taking part in a science club, doing more than required for homework (or, at the very least, doing all that is required well), reading science books/magazines, watching science programmes on television, viewing science based websites, visiting places of scientific interest and the like.

By comparing the claims regarding the motivational value of practical work, with pupils' actions both in and out of the laboratory, and their stated intentions as to whether they intend to pursue science in the post-compulsory phase of their education, provides a useful means of appraising the extent to which such claims are supported by the evidence. If, as has been claimed (Hannon, 1994; Lazarowitz and Tamir, 1994; Ames, 1992; Henry, 1975), practical work does motivate then, given that biology arguably offers the least amount of practical work of the three sciences, it might be expected that it would be the least popular science to be pursued post-compulsion. Yet the findings of the House of Commons Science and Technology Committee (2002) suggest that in fact the converse is true and 'the proportion of A level entries accounted for by chemistry and physics is falling...while biology has largely retained its popularity' (p. 23). Echoing this point a head of department in this study (Mr Normanby) drew specific attention to the fact that 'more of our pupils do biology [at A-level] although, if I'm not mistaken, there is a lot less practical work in biology [at Key Stages 3 and 4] than in say chemistry or even physics'. A similar, albeit more general, point was made by another teacher (Mr Saltmarsh) who claimed that 'A lot of kids that I teach do probably less practical in biology than any other of the sciences but a lot of them prefer biology to chemistry and physics'. Logically speaking it could be argued that without the frequent use of practical work in chemistry and physics throughout Key Stages 3 and 4 the number of pupils pursuing these two subjects might be even lower than it currently is. However, we need to be aware that the increased use of practical work that accompanied the Nuffield inspired changes to the curriculum during the 1960's did not, as Hodson (1990) has pointed out, result in any increase in the number of pupils choosing to pursue science post compulsion, as might have been expected had practical work been an effective motivating factor. Similarly a report by the Department of Education and Science (1968) (The Dainton Report), produced at a time when Nuffield inspired changes to the curriculum might have been expected to increase the uptake of science at 'A' level, found that the number of pupils pursuing science at this level had actually *decreased* – a finding that subsequently became known as the 'swing from science'.

That said, as you will probably be aware, there is a need to recognize that the educational system in England, in which pupils are required to specialize at the end of Key Stage 4, must result in some pupils not pursuing their study of science because of positive choices in favour of other subjects, rather than negative views of, or a lack of motivation towards, science. However, the old adage that 'actions speak louder than words' lends credence to the claim by Bennett (2003) that, while certain practical tasks can generate interest and/or engagement within a particular lesson, there is little evidence to suggest that they motivate pupils towards science in general or even towards one, or more, of the sciences in particular.

Interest

Prenzel (1992) suggests that the term 'interest', as commonly used, 'describes preferences for objects' (p. 73), where the term 'objects' is used in a very broad sense as, for example, when someone claims to have an interest in sport. Within the psychological literature the term 'interest' is used more precisely to refer to 'a person's interaction with a *specific* class of tasks, objects, events, or ideas' (Krapp et al., 1992, p. 8. Italics in original). An example of which would be the interest shown by some people in solving cryptic crosswords. While it has been claimed (Hidi and Harackiewicz, 2000) that this description of interest is widely accepted, many psychological theorists make a distinction between what have been termed 'personal' and 'situational' interest (Hidi and Harackiewicz, 2000; Bergin, 1999). In order to evaluate what is actually meant by claims that 'practical work generates interest' it is necessary to understand that these two types of interest differ appreciably from one another and that each has its own set of characteristics.

Personal interest

Personal interest, sometimes referred to as 'individual' interest, is primarily concerned with the relative ranking of an individual's preferences. Indeed, as Bergin (1999) makes clear, the 'individual approach [to interest] asks what dispositional preferences people hold, or what *enduring* preferences they have for certain activities or domains of knowledge' (p. 87. Italics added). Studies in the area of personal interest such as those by Renninger (1998) and Schiefele

(1996) have found that children who undertake a particular activity, or study a subject, in which they already have a personal interest will, compared to children with no prior personal interest, be observed to pay closer attention to, learn more from, and engage for longer with, any new material that they are presented with. The relationship between personal interest in, and knowledge of, a subject or activity arises because individuals prefer, when given a choice, to study what already interests them (Bergin, 1999). By increasing their knowledge of that subject, or activity, they increase their personal interest in it yet further (Alexander, 1997; Alexander et al., 1995) developing what we might usefully think of as a system of positive feedback.

There are numerous factors that can stimulate personal interest. Bergin (1999) suggests relevance, competence, identification, cultural value, social support, background knowledge and emotions, all of which are, generally speaking, beyond a teacher's immediate domain of influence. While personal interest can be an important factor in effective learning (Schiefele et al., 1992), one that is characterized by positive feelings towards, and an increased knowledge of, a subject or activity (Bergin, 1999; Schiefele, 1998), it is not something that is, in the short term at least, susceptible to teacher influence (Hidi and Harackiewicz, 2000).

Situational interest

Situational interest refers to the interest that is stimulated in individuals as a consequence of their being in a particular environment or situation (Hidi and Harackiewicz, 2000; Bergin, 1999; Krapp et al., 1992) such as, for example, when your pupils undertake a practical task within a science laboratory. Unlike personal interest, situational interest *is* susceptible to teacher influence in the short term (Hidi and Berdorff, 1998; Hidi and Anderson, 1992). While it is far less likely than personal interest to endure over time (Hidi and Harackiewicz, 2000; Murphy and Alexander, 2000), it does provide an opportunity for a teacher to influence the effectiveness of their pupils' learning in specific lessons in a positive manner (Hoffmann and Häussler, 1998; Mitchell, 1993). Furthermore, it has been suggested (Hidi and Harackiewicz, 2000; Hidi 1990) that the stimulation of situational interest would be of the greatest benefit in influencing learning among those pupils with little or no personal interest.

While this distinction, between personal and situational interest, is useful in considering the type of interest that practical work might stimulate, you need to remember that while personal interest is relatively stable, and hence resistant to your influence, it is not totally immune to situational influences. In discussing the generation of personal interest Bergin (1999) stresses that 'personal or individual factors always interact with situational factors to create interest, or lack of interest' (p. 89). Hidi and Harackiewicz (2000) illustrate this interaction by way of the following example:

> [S]tudents who are exposed to an exciting lecture in psychology may be stimulated and pay more attention in class than they ever have before. For some students, this interest may evaporate as soon as the lecture ends. For others, the interest triggered in this situation persist over time and may develop into individual [personal] interest in psychology. (p. 155)

Despite the possible role of practical work in stimulating situational interest there has, as yet, been no specific research to ascertain what particular situational factors, if any, make a practical task appear more, or less, interesting to pupils. To date, the only studies that have been undertaken on the issue of how to increase pupil interest have been those that have examined the factors that influence the degree of situational interest stimulated by different types of text (Hidi and Anderson, 1992; Hidi, 1990; Wade and Adams, 1990; Garner et al., 1989). These studies have shown that situational interest is stimulated to a greater extent by texts that were characterized by the researchers as surprising, vivid, intense and novel. In the area of practical work similar characteristics for memorable episodes have been reported (Abrahams, 2009; White, 1996, 1991).

You need also to be aware that while it has been reported that pupils' themselves claim to *like* practical work (Ben-Zvi et al., 1977; Hofstein, et al., 1976; Henry, 1975), or that teachers' – and here you might well include yourself – claim that their pupils *like* practical work (Bryant and Marek, 1987; Jakeways, 1986), such claims do not necessarily imply that the pupils are in fact *interested* in it. This is very significant in that while a necessary feature of any personal interest in a subject, or activity, is the need for the individual to also like that particular subject or activity (Schiefele, 1991), this is not necessarily the case for situational interest in which an 'interest in' and 'liking of' a subject can arise independently of each other (Hidi and Anderson, 1992). This independence is nicely illustrated by Iran-Nejad (1987) who notes that a 'snake can be interesting without being liked, and a particular soft drink may be liked without being interesting' (p. 121).

Having distinguished between 'interest in' and 'liking of', I would point out also that 'interest in' doing a particular practical task – as evidenced by your pupils' apparent involvement with the objects, materials and phenomena – does not (unfortunately) imply, as many teachers appear to believe it does, cognitive engagement with any, or all, of the intended ideas or concepts.

Blumenfeld and Meece (1988) have reported finding that pupils could be fully engaged and seemingly interested in what they were *doing* without their being cognitively engaged with the task in a manner that would have been necessary for them to have learnt what the teacher intended. This suggests that, in terms of the two domains of knowledge discussed earlier, pupils may be interested only (or mainly) in the objects, materials and phenomena and not the ideas. As Kerr (1964) reports 'We were repeatedly told by teachers and students that they had been so engrossed in what they were *doing* and how it was done that they had given little thought to why they did it' (p. 20. Italics added). Along similar lines Bergin (1999) has cautioned that although 'most teachers aspire to increase the interest of their students, they should keep in mind the fact that interest enhancement does not necessarily lead to learning enhancement' (p. 96).

Having distinguished between motivation and interest, personal interest and situational interest, as well as between an 'interest in' and a 'liking of' practical work, I now want to consider the value of practical work in the affective domain.

Pupils claim to like practical work

Almost all of the pupils questioned in this study said that they liked practical work. However, when these responses were probed further, during discussions with the pupils, it was found that in many cases it was not that the pupils actually liked practical work per se – although some pupils in Year 7 did appear to and I will return to these later – but rather that they liked it *better* than most alternative, non-practical, methods of teaching science. In contrast to Head (1982), who reported finding a small but significant number of pupils who expressed a dislike of practical work, in this study of those pupils questioned only 1 claimed to dislike practical work, because they found it boring, while 96 claimed, for various reasons, to like it. Pupils' reasons for claiming to like practical work are presented in Table 2.1 in which there are two types of claim: those indicative of a relative preference (containing comparative terms such as; better than, less than, more than), and what might be termed 'absolute' claims (such as: it is fun, it is exciting, I just like it). An asterisk indicates all relative preferences.

Of the 96 claims, 65 (68%) are indicative of a 'relative' preference for practical work, while 31 (32%) are 'absolute'. In order to analyse whether there were any trends in the views expressed by pupils about practical work that alter with age, Tables 2.2 and 2.3 show the breakdown of their 'absolute' and 'relative' preferences by Year groups.

Table 2.1 Pupils' reasons for claiming to like practical work

Pupils' reasons for claiming to like practical work	Number of pupils (N=96) offering such a response
*Because it is less boring than writing	47
Because it is fun	16
Because you get to make/do things	10
*Because it is better than listening to the teacher	4
*Because you will remember it better	3
*Because it is better than reading from a textbook	3
*Because you learn more	3
Because you can see what happens	2
*Because it helps you understand Better	2
Because you get to find things out	1
*Because it is better than theory	1
Because it is exciting	1
*Because it is more believable	1
Because you gain an experience	1
*Because it is better than work	1

Table 2.2 Pupil's 'absolute' responses by Year group

Response type 'absolute'	Year 7	Year 8	Year 9	Year 10	Year 11
Because it is fun	8	3	1	3	1
Because you get to make/do things	4	3	1	2	0
Because you can see what happens	0	1	0	1	0
Because you gain an experience	0	1	0	0	0
Because it is exciting	1	0	0	0	0
Because you get to find things out	1	0	0	0	0
Total number of responses	**14**	**8**	**2**	**6**	**1**

Table 2.3 Pupil's 'relative' responses by Year group

Response type 'relative'	Year 7	Year 8	Year 9	Year 10	Year 11
Because it is less boring than writing	12	15	6	10	4
Because it is better than listening to the teacher	0	3	0	1	0
Because you will remember it better	0	0	0	1	2
Because it is better than reading from a textbook	0	2	0	0	1
Because you learn more	0	1	1	1	0
Because it helps you understand better	0	0	0	2	0
Because it is better than theory	0	0	0	1	0
Because it is more believable	0	1	0	0	0
Because it is better than work	0	1	0	0	0
Total number of responses	**12**	**23**	**7**	**16**	**7**

Table 2.4 A comparison of 'absolute' and 'relative' responses by Year group

Group	Number of 'absolute' responses	Number of 'relative' responses	Percentage (%) of 'absolute' responses	Percentage (%) of 'relative' responses
Year 7	14	12	54	46
Year 8	8	23	26	74
Year 9	2	7	22	78
Year 10	6	16	27	73
Year 11	1	8	13	87

While there are no obvious patterns in Tables 2.2 and 2.3 you can see that the claims 'because it is less boring than writing' and 'because it is fun' were the most common 'relative' and 'absolute' responses respectively in every Year group.

While the sample size (N = 96) is relatively small, and not all Year groups are equally represented, it is still possible to compare the proportion of 'absolute' and 'relative' responses given by pupils in each Year group and these results are presented in Table 2.4.

What emerges clearly from Table 2.4 is that after Year 7, in which the majority of pupil responses were 'absolute', the situation reverses to one in which the majority of claims, to like practical work, have become statements of relative preference that stays much the same in Years 8, 9 and 10 before shifting even further towards 'relative' in Year 11. One possible explanation for this is that among Year 7 pupils many of these practical tasks provide the first opportunity to use scientific equipment and/or materials and this is something that the pupils appear to like in an 'absolute' sense. Many Year 7 pupils spoke excitedly simply about being allowed to use standard pieces of laboratory equipment and/or materials such as Bunsen burners, electrical wire and acids – something that was not observed among pupils in later Years. The following extracts are a sample of the comments made by Year 7 pupils and I would expect that you will have heard similar enthusiastic comments from your own Year 7 pupils.

FS11: At the beginning of the year we got red cabbage liquid and . . .
FS10: [Interrupting.] Yeah it was great fun.
FS11: We was adding acid to it and different kinds of real chemicals and seeing what colour it turns stuff. It were fun.

Researcher: Do you like practical work?
KG5: Yeah because we get to use proper wire for the first time and we get to use a six vec *(sic)* [volt] battery thing which is very powerful.

> Researcher: Do you like practical work?
> KN9: Yeah.
> Researcher: Why?
> KN9: Because you get to make things and do exciting experiments that are exciting.
> KN11: And at primary school you didn't get to do anything exciting.
> Researcher: You didn't? So you come to secondary school and you can do exciting practical work.
> KN9: We did experiments, but nothing that involved Bunsen burners.

What the data in Table 2.4 suggest is that an 'absolute' liking of practical work, that arises out of the fun, enjoyment and excitement that pupils appear to associate with using new equipment and/or materials in what is a novel environment – the science laboratory – starts to wane, for many pupils, during the latter part of their first year at secondary school. While the onset of a decline in pupil interest in science from Year 7 onwards has been reported (Bennett, 2003; Doherty and Dawe, 1988; Johnson, 1987), the fact that almost half (46%) of the Year 7 claims (Table 2.4) were already claims of relative preference lends credence to the findings of Pell and Jarvis (2001) which suggest that a decline in interest may start *before* pupils reach secondary school.

Because many pupils do not appear, especially after Year 7, to *like* practical work in itself, the interest that it generates when you use it seems best understood as being situational rather than personal. As situational interest will not persist beyond the practical lesson itself it can be seen that unless you make regular use of practical work – to re-stimulate situational interest – your pupils will perceive science, and/or non-practical science lessons, as boring, *despite* your having used practical work on numerous previous occasions. The following extracts illustrate how an underlying view that science is 'boring' emerges as soon as it is suggested that practical work, the source of situational interest, be either reduced or removed from science lessons:

> Researcher: What would you think about science if you didn't have practicals?
> RH6: Boring. [Said in a very slow drawn out manner.]
> RH7: Boring. [Said in a very slow drawn out manner.]
>
>

Researcher: How do you think a science lesson would be if it didn't have much practical?

SY3: Well for the majority of last year we didn't have much practical and it got really boring and it started getting [*sic*] complaints to the teacher.

Researcher: What would science be like without practical?

FY14: Boring.

FY15: Yeah most of the time.

Researcher: What do you think science would be like if there was less practical?

KD13: Boring. If you come in and there's no practical it's not as fun, you're just sitting down writing stuff from the textbook.

Such views suggest that while practical work can stimulate situational interest this is not being translated, as the following examples illustrate, into a personal, and enduring, interest in science – one that can be maintained without the continual need for regular practical work.

Researcher: Do you like doing practical work?

SK15: Yeah.

Researcher: Why?

SK18: 'cause it's fun.

Researcher: Would you hope to do any of the sciences after GCSE?

SK18: No not really.

SK19: No nor me.

Researcher: Why's that?

SK18: I'm not into science.

Researcher: Have you enjoyed this practical?

SK28: Yeah it was all right; it wasn't as fun as other ones we've had though.

Researcher: Are you going to take science at 'A' level?

SK28: No not really I'm not really in to it all.

Researcher: But you did say you liked practical.

SK28: Yeah but, 'cause sometimes it's fun, and practical's easier than, well, writing.

Claims, such as these, suggest that some pupils perceive the liking of practical work as separate to, and distinct from, a liking of science. As Kelly (1986) points out, 'science' is used as a generic term for biology, chemistry and physics, and, therefore, pupils' liking for each specific science may be very different. Furthermore, you also need to be aware that pupils' preference for practical work *within* science does not necessarily equate to a preference for science over other school subjects. And while there has been relatively little research into subject preferences among pupils (Osborne et al., 2003) dispositional preferences are an indication of personal interest (Bergin, 1999) and, as such, can show us how a pupil's personal interest in one subject compares with their interest in another. Whitefield (1980) has found that when pupils were asked to rank their liking of school subjects (practical work in science was not considered separately) chemistry and physics, the two sciences that arguably offer the most practical work, were among the least popular school subjects. Yet biology, the school science that arguably provides the least amount of practical work, was ranked as one of the most popular subjects (Whitefield, 1980). The point that I want to emphasize here is that neither the amount of practical work you do, or your pupils' preference for it, seems to provide an explanation for the relative popularity (or otherwise) of the subjects. One possible explanation for this is that while pupils might prefer practical work they are, as the House of Commons Science and Technology Committee (2002) has reported, 'frequently motivated by a longer term ambition to follow a particular career' (p. 23). Indeed, the following example illustrates how one pupil's future career aspiration, rather than their preference for a particular subject (chemistry), influences their choice to pursue biology and not chemistry during the post-compulsory phase of their education.

Researcher: Are any of you three planning on doing science after GCSE?
SK27: No.
SK25: No.
SK26: I might, might probably do biology because I want to do something in sport.
Researcher: Do you like doing practical?
SK25: Yeah.
SK27: Yeah, me too.
SK26: I prefer chemistry to any of the other sciences.
Researcher: Why?
SK26: I find it more interesting, I just like the practical lesson bits, the experiments you do.
Researcher: Do you like the practicals in biology?
SK26: They're all right; I don't mind them.
Researcher: What's different about the practicals in chemistry and the practicals in biology?

SK26: Well, it's like sorta, chemical reactions.

SK25: Well you can do more practicals in chemistry can't you.

SK26: Yeah and there's explosions and fires and stuff like that.

Researcher: [To SK26] But now you've said you'd like to study biology.

SK26: Ah yeah, but I'm thinking about what I want to do in later life.

Again career requirements, rather than the amount of practical work, were also, as the following example illustrates, found to be more influential in determining which of the science subjects to pursue post-compulsion.

Researcher: Which science do you like best?

KD1: Biology.

KD2: Biology.

Researcher: Which science has the least practical in it?

KD1: Biology.

KD2: Yeah.

Researcher: So the fact that you like biology has got no connection to the amount of practical?

KD2: But if I want to be a nurse I need to do biology.

KD1: Yeah, and I want to be a vet.

Although preference ranking does not provide an absolute measure of a pupil's liking for a particular subject or activity (Osborne et al., 2003), it does provide a means of comparing an individual's personal interest in a range of subjects and/or activities and – given the claims as to the motivational value of practical work (Hannon, 1994; Lazarowitz and Tamir, 1994; Ames, 1992; Henry, 1975) – of exploring how personal interest in subjects relates to the amount of practical work that are offered in those subjects.

Researcher: How do you rate practical work compared to other things that you do at school?

DX4: I think practical work is better than English because you get to do stuff and experiment and you don't have to write stuff down.

Researcher: If someone said to you that you could do practical science or you could do P.E. what would you do?

⇨

NK16: P.E.
NK15: P.E.
Researcher: Practical science or geography?
NK16: Practical science.
NK15: Practical science 'cause geography's boring.
Researcher: Practical science or English?
NK16: English because we do other stuff. [On later questioning this 'other stuff' was found to be drama.]
NK15: I don't know which one I'd do.

The implication here is that even when pupils claim to prefer science *practical work* to other subjects, and it must be emphasized here that the preference is not for science as a subject but only for the practical work component within it, their reasons for doing so appear, unfortunately, to have little to do with personal interest in the subject per se. Many of you who already teach science, or are training to teach science, will be aware of pupils who, while claiming to find practical work interesting, fun and enjoyable, lack any motivation to do more than the minimum required of them and, as the following example illustrates, show no interest in science as a subject.

Researcher: Do you think that practical work encourages you to study science?
SY13: Yeah.
Researcher: Are you going to study science after GCSE?
SY13: Definitely not.

Generally speaking pupils do not like practical work per se (Abrahams, 2005; Edwards and Power, 1990; Gardner and Gould, 1990; Hodson, 1990; Denney and Chennell, 1986; Hofstein and Lunetta, 1982). Rather, as Hodson (1990) notes, they 'regard practical work as a "less boring" alternative to other methods' (p. 34). Because personal interest entails a liking of the subject or activity for itself the kind of liking that leads to preferring practical work to non-practical alternatives is likely to produce, at best, situational interest.

Another way to look at the data in Table 2.1 is to divide the reasons pupils gave for liking practical work into three broad categories:

(i) Reasons that related to their affective response to practical work.
(ii) Reasons that related to doing things with objects and ideas.
(iii) Reasons that related to learning about objects and ideas.

Table 2.5 The distribution of the pupil responses in terms of three generic categories (N = 96)

Generic category of response	Pupils' reasons for claiming to like practical work	Number of pupils offering such a response
Reasons that related to the affective value of practical work	Because it is less boring than writing Because it is fun Because it is better than listening to the teacher Because it is better than reading from a textbook Because it is better than theory Because it is exciting Because it is more believable Because it is better than work	73
Reasons relating to making, doing and seeing.	Because you get to make/do things Because you can see what happens Because you get to find things out Because you gain an experience	17
Reasons relating to learning, understanding and recollecting	Because you will remember it better Because you learn more Because it helps you understand better	6

Table 2.5 illustrates the distribution of the pupil responses in terms of each of these three broad categories.

As Table 2.5 shows, claims in the broad 'affective' category constitute the largest group of reasons given by pupils for liking practical work, accounting for 76 per cent of all responses. It should, however, be pointed out that some of the reasons for liking practical work within this category, as the following quotation illustrates, are less of a positive endorsement of practical work than a desire to avoid having to write and/or do too much work:

Researcher: Do you like practical work?

SW1: Yeah it's better than doing other work.

Researcher: What other work?

SW1: Like writing.

Researcher: Do you think this is going to be an exciting experiment?

SW1: Well it's not exactly exciting but it's better than working all the time in the lesson.

Researcher: Do you think this particular practical helps you in any way?

SW1: No, it's just less boring.

Certainly this pupil's view, that practical work did not involve *working* all of the time, supports a view expressed by one teacher (Mrs Ugthorpe) who, when asked why she thought practical work was popular among pupils, stated that 'I think it's [practical work] just an easy option'. Likewise Mr Normanby, a head of department, expressed a similar view when he claimed that the popularity of practical work among pupils was in part due to the fact that it avoided their 'having to think'. That pupils prefer the 'easy option' gains support from another head of department (Mr Rainton) who suggested that subject choice appeared to have little to do with the amount of practical work offered, or its affective value, since 'When you ask kids why they're doing these subjects [non-science "A" levels] they just say it's easier, that's it, end of story'. Such views support earlier findings that pupils' decisions not to pursue science are influenced strongly by their perception of science as difficult (Hendley et al., 1996) and that perceived difficulty can be the main factor in dissuading pupils from deciding to study science at 'A' level (Harvard, 1996).

Of the remaining pupils, 18 per cent cited, as their reason for liking practical work, issues relating to making, doing and seeing, while only 6 per cent claimed that they liked it because it helped them to learn, understand and recollect ideas and concepts. What these findings suggest is that despite many of the pupils claiming to like practical work better than non-practical alternatives – in particular writing – very few pupils saw it, as has also been reported by Cerini et al., (2003), as a better way of learning about, and understanding, scientific ideas and concepts.

Having looked at pupils' views regarding the affective value of practical work I now want to consider the views of science teachers.

Science teachers' views on the affective value of practical work

While some teachers initially used the term 'motivation' when talking about the value of practical work it emerged, during further discussions with these teachers, that in all but one case – that of Mr Ulleskelf – they were using the term 'motivate' to mean the generation of situational interest – or what some teachers referred to as 'short-term engagement'. The following examples are illustrative of this:

Researcher: If then, at one end of a scale, practical work was said to motivate pupils towards science in general and towards the pursuit of science post Key Stage 4 and

> at the other end to engage pupils in a particular lesson, where would you place practical work?
> Mr Keld: I think it's the particular lesson.
>
> Researcher: If motivation is a continuum where at one end practical work could be thought of as inspiring an interest towards science and at the other end we might talk about getting pupils involved or engaged in a particular lesson, where would you think that particular practical would fall?
> Mrs Uckerby: It motivated them in that lesson, it got them involved in thinking about circuit diagrams, which they haven't done for a long time, which they couldn't remember. It wouldn't influence them into taking physics up as a career.

Mr Ulleskelf was the only teacher who indicated that his use of the term 'motivation' meant more than just the generation of non-enduring situational interest within a particular lesson.

> Mr Ulleskelf: But it does have a motivating effect on most [academic ability] groups.
> Researcher: Now when you say motivating do you mean encouraging pupils to go beyond the requirements of the syllabus, to enhance their curiosity and understanding about science or whether, by motivation, you mean it gets them engaged in that particular lesson and therefore it's important to have practical frequently otherwise they lose the sense of engagement?
> Mr Ulleskelf: Both, but it's the latter one that's more important in terms of actually getting across a piece of information and getting the understanding, particularly with your lower [academic] ability sets.

Once it is recognized that the term 'motivating' is frequently used by teachers not to imply 'an inner drive to action' (Bandura, 1986 p. 243) but rather what, in psychological terms, would be referred to as situational interest, the effect of which would be unlikely to endure beyond that particular lesson *the need continually to re-stimulate the pupils' through the regular use of practical work, becomes more understandable*. It might be argued at this point that the fact that pupils regularly request to do practical work, exemplifies the motivational value of practical work and that its frequent use is designed to enhance the effect. However, the fact that teachers report that the absence of practical work, even for a few lessons among pupils who have been undertaking regular practical work for almost five years, made them behaviourally harder to manage suggests that its affective value is better understood in terms of its generating non-enduring situational interest than any form of enduring motivation towards science as a subject.

The value of situational interest

Having suggested that what many teachers might refer to as motivation is, in fact, situational interest, I want now to consider why you, as a science teacher, might still want to generate what is essentially a non-enduring form of interest. What emerges from discussions with teachers is that they perceive practical work as having two, very distinct, affective purposes:

(i) To help in the behavioural management of the class – particularly with low to low/middle academic ability pupils.
(ii) To help off-set the image of science as difficult, dull and boring by presenting an alternative image of science in which the emphasis is primarily on 'doing' fun and enjoyable 'hands-on' work rather than on learning about ideas.

It is to a consideration of these two purposes that I now turn.

The role of practical work in behaviour management

Some of the comments made by the teachers suggest that while pupils frequently arrive at science lessons with the expectation, or at least a hope, that they will be able to do practical work those keenest on doing practical work are often pupils of low academic ability who have no intention of pursuing science post compulsion. For many of these pupils the hope of doing practical work appears to owe more to their desire to avoid writing (Table 2.1) than any genuine personal interest in doing practical work. This desire, on the part of pupils, to avoid writing is frequently recognized, and commented upon, by teachers. The following extracts are examples of these comments.

Mrs Duggleby: I think all people have got this idea about science and practical work. Ok practical work and they [these other people], if you say 'practical work for kids' they will just go 'yes that's fantastic and engaging' but I think there's an element of 'well we [the pupils] don't like writing down and so we want to get on and do something like that'.

I think there are so many other subjects in school where they're writing that anything that's practically orientated they'd prefer to do that.

> Dr Kepwick: It is a carrot with them [academically low ability pupils], it is more about making it bearable. For them it's just less writing. I think higher ability pupils could get by with fewer practicals but [non-practical science lessons would] still engage and interest them.

One teacher (Miss Sharow) saw the teaching of non-practical science lessons in a laboratory as problematic in that laboratories, unlike classrooms, are essentially designed, with their uncomfortable stools, and benches containing sinks, power points and gas taps, for *doing* rather than sitting and writing (Donnelly, 1998).

> Miss Sharow: I think the whole thing generates an expectation for practical work [gestures around the laboratory], just the lab, you know, the gas taps, the water taps. So when they come in and it's not a normal classroom, you know, if they were sitting in a normal classroom, you know, they'd be thinking, you know, 'alright, we're not going to do practical because there's nothing to use.' Where as they come in here and see all the equipment out at the back [points to equipment at the back of the laboratory], gas taps and, you know, I think being in the lab raises expectations of practical work.

Whether the pupils' expectations and/or hopes to undertake practical work in science lessons are driven by a genuine personal interest in practical work, or merely by a desire to avoid having to write, what is clear is that these expectations and/or hopes are nonetheless real. Therefore what is important, especially from your own perspective, is the question of how your pupils react to those lessons, or sequences of lessons, in which their expectations and/or hopes to do practical work are not fulfilled. Among the teachers in this study what emerges, as the following examples show, is a widespread perception that without interspersing practical work into a teaching sequence, on a frequent and regular basis, pupils become not only uninterested but also noticeably more difficult to manage, in terms of their behaviour, during non-practical lessons:

> Researcher: And if you say no [to doing practical work]?
> Miss Sharow: Murrrrr. [Pulls a face that appears to indicate something unpleasant.]
>

Researcher: So do you find it makes it harder for you as a teacher if you can't give them practical?

Miss Sharow: Yeah, that's what I'd say. [Nodding head vigorously in agreement.] It's certainly like that with some of the classes like that.

[Year 11 – weakest academic ability class.]

Mr Normanby: The kids soon work out which teacher gives more practical work and certainly, for most classes, two lessons of theory on the trot is about the limit, after that they'll be very hard to teach. It's carrot and stick really.

Mr Saltmarsh: They come with the hope that they are going to do practical.
Researcher: If they don't get practical?
Mr Saltmarsh: It can be awkward.

Mr Drax: You know, as soon as they come through the door they're asking 'Sir are we doing practical today?' If I say 'no' I've lost them even before they sit down. If I say 'yes' I can keep their interest and, although they still might not learn anything, they will be easier to deal with.

Mr Rainton: At least they'll be engaged and it'll prevent them from any sort of disruption of any kind. It will allow the other kids, who are on the sidelines, to actually progress and do some work [without disruption].

This last point, made by Mr Rainton, was echoed by Mrs Ramsgill who, when interviewed after a lesson in which a number of academically low ability pupils had continuously misbehaved and disrupted the learning of others in the class, pointed out that:

Mrs Ramsgill: It's hard to get anything done when they [the disruptive pupils] don't feel like doing practical work.
Researcher: Would non-practical have been easier?
Mrs Ramsgill: No [screws up her eyes and shakes her head], that'd have been even worse.

Another teacher (Mr Keld) claimed that to cope with poor behaviour among Year 10 pupils, behaviour that he attributed to their not having undertaken practical work for a *few* lessons, that was disrupting a non-practical lesson, he had felt obliged to say to them '"You haven't done any practical, I know you like doing it, and there's going to be two next week. So if you can just keep going with the theory this week." So I don't try to sell it to them but I do let them know that there's a light at the end of the tunnel'. Similarly Mrs Duggleby reported using the possibility of practical work later in the lesson 'as a carrot, you know, "can you be quiet please because we're going to do some practical"'.

Taken together these claims suggest that for many of the teachers, particularly those involved in teaching science to pupils of low academic ability who have little, if any, personal interest in science, there was a concern about the need to establish and maintain what Brown and McIntyre (1993) refer to as a 'Normal Desirable State of Pupil Activity (NDS)' (p. 54). Furthermore, there is an understanding that the frequent use of practical work, irrespective of how effective it is in terms of achieving the desired learning objectives, is an effective strategy for coping with poor behaviour. Certainly the view expressed by Richmond (1978) that 'Most physics teachers would answer the question "Who Needs Laboratories?" with the answer "I do"' (p. 49) was echoed by Mrs Ramsgill who claimed 'It [the use of practical work] can make my life easier'.

If practical and non-practical work are equally effective (or ineffective) in terms of developing conceptual understanding then the very fact that, as one teacher (Mr Drax) suggests, the use of practical work means that 'I can keep their interest and, although they still might not learn anything, they will be easier to deal with' provides a pragmatic justification for using practical work. Yet in order for practical work to be effective in getting pupils of all academic abilities to do, and see, what you intended the practical tasks will invariably be of a closed 'recipe' style. The advantage of these, as Kirschner (1992) notes, is that 'Years of effort have produced "foolproof" experiments where the right answer is certain to emerge for everyone in the class if the laboratory instructions are followed' (p. 278).

It should therefore come as no surprise to you to find academically low ability pupils exhibiting their displeasure, through poor behaviour, when required to write and/or think for themselves about scientific ideas rather than simply being allowed to *do* a cognitively undemanding 'recipe' style practical task.

Certainly for some teachers there was, as the following extracts illustrate, a perception that for some low academic ability pupils practical work was essentially just 'something for them to *do*' in order to make both their time, and therefore hopefully the teachers' time, bearable. In such cases there appeared to be little, if any, expectation on the part of the teacher that any meaningful learning would occur:

Miss Sharow: I mean some of the ones we've got are very weak and they're so weak they can't even do the calculations, you know, so they can't even plot the graph, you know, it's [practical work] just something to do with them.

Mr Rainton: Because, if nothing else, it's [practical work] a relief, it's something different they're doing.

Mrs Ramsgill: It [practical work] gives them something to do, especially the ones who get bored with too much writing

'Recipe' style practical tasks do appear to be a relatively effective means of keeping most of the pupils engaged during a lesson. However, I would suggest that its use helps to generate a liking, not for science per se, but for a specific part of science – practical work – in which the emphasis is primarily on doing with objects, materials and phenomena rather than learning about ideas. Some teachers consider their use of practical work as a 'carrot' and it seems reasonable to assume that, in this context, it is non-practical 'theory' that constitutes the 'stick'. It is not surprising, given such a 'carrot' and 'stick' approach to practical and non-practical work, that pupils appear reluctant to engage with the 'theory', or 'stick', side of the subject in a manner that would be necessary if science teaching and learning was to be 'an interplay between experiment and theory' (Millar, 1991 p. 43).

The role of practical work in helping to foster a view of science as fun, exciting and enjoyable

One of the most disappointing things I think, from a science teacher's perspective, is the fact that pupils, from as early as the end of Year 7, have moved from claiming to like practical work in an 'absolute' sense to merely preferring it to other non-practical teaching methods and approaches (Table 2.4). One factor that might help explain this change in pupils' perceptions is, I believe, related to how science is initially portrayed to Year 6 pupils when they visit secondary schools on Open Days and Open Evening. During such visits these Year 6 pupils are often encouraged by the teachers to 'see' (Ogborn et al., 1996) science as being primarily a fun, exciting and enjoyable *practical* activity:

Mr Keld: We'll do things that are the most interesting, so we try to sell it. The whole ethos behind Open Evening that is put down from the top of the school, from the SMT [Senior Management Team] through the head of department to us, is it wants to be interesting and good, and good fun.

Mrs Kettlesing: On Open Evening we always do whiz, bang, pops. The only physics thing we have out is the van de Graaff.
Researcher: What do you think then of this image of science as being all whiz, bang, pops?
Mrs Kettlesing: Maybe we're giving a false picture, I think we are probably. There aren't that many whiz bang, pops and most science is really about how does the world work and testing things out, why is this happening, why is that happening, rather than whiz bang, pops

When asked to explain the purpose of such an approach Mrs Kettlesing suggested that the reason was that 'We're trying to make it appear more exciting, I suppose because it isn't exciting all of the time'. It should also be noted that Mrs Uckerby, when questioned about the use of practical tasks on Open Days, expressed views that were very similar:

Researcher: Can I ask what you do on Open Days?

Mrs Uckerby: Do you mean how or what?

Researcher: What you actually do.

Mrs Uckerby: Each science puts on a selection of practicals and pupils, and their parents, wander around and try them out.

Researcher: What type of practicals do you use?

Mrs Uckerby: We try to use something eye catching and exciting and it's important, I think, that the kids find it fun.

Researcher: What would you do in physics?

Mrs Uckerby: I tend to have the van de Graaff out. The kids, and parents love it, although what with health and safety that will sadly probably have to go. But I also like imploding drinks cans and making plasticine boats to support as many coins as possible.

Researcher: Do you feel that is representative of practical work in general?

Mrs Uckerby: Definitely not [laughing] but I've got to compete with biology's dissection and, I mean, how often do they do dissections?

These quotations suggest that many science teachers recognize that practical work is not, generally speaking, fun and exciting and that there are only a limited number of practical tasks – the 'whiz' 'bang' 'pops' – that can be used on Open Days, or the like, when such an image needs (or is required) to be presented. The atypical nature of such tasks was also evident in a letter from the head of science at Ouse School, to head teachers of local primary feeder schools, regarding the itinerary for a Year 6 'Science (chemistry) in Action Day' in which it was stated that the pupils would spend the day 'making Chemical Worms, Bouncing Custard, Chemical Gardens and the *usual* explosions' (Italics added). While it would be possible for the pupils to learn something about the scientific ideas associated with these tasks it seems more likely, given that the event was only to last two hours, that these practical activities were chosen to present a particular image of science. It must be emphasized that I (as a physics teacher) am not suggesting that science is never fun, exciting and enjoyable (far from it) but that such an image does not truthfully reflect 'normal' school science. One teacher (Miss Kilburn) saw the main problem as being that 'normal' school science was simply not sufficiently exciting for enough of the time:

> Miss Kilburn: I think a main problem is that we don't do enough exciting stuff and lots of them have got bored by Year 10 and 11 just when we'd ideally want them to be switched on to science because they're bored of dull experiments that look at how springs stretch as you add more weight, but that's what we've got to do, it's such a pity really.

Another teacher (Mr Fangfoss) suggested that it was the quantity rather than quality of practical work that was important particularly among low academic ability pupils who were not expected to pursue science post compulsion:

> Mr Fangfoss: We try to give them [academically low ability pupils] as much practical work as possible so that they will remember science as being enjoyable and interesting.

Although this view was expressed by only one teacher it suggests that when practical work is used with pupils of low academic ability your aim might not necessarily be to motivate them to study science beyond Key Stage 4 but rather to provide them with a positive recollection of the subject. The clear implication, if this view is taken to its logical conclusion, is that it becomes more important for you to ensure that the pupils enjoy their lessons, irrespective of whether they learn or not, and that the best way to achieve this is to maximize the amount of time spent 'doing' practical work.

Some teachers appear, as the following examples serve to illustrate, to draw on their own positive recollections of studying science at school in order to justify the affective value of practical work:

> Miss Kilburn: I was lucky really because when I was at school my science teacher ran a science club at lunch time and, even now, I can remember us all getting shocks from the van de Graaff. It made it so much fun.
> Mr Fangfoss: I still remember dissecting a rabbit and enjoying doing it.

Here it is important for you to recognize just how atypical you are, not only from an academic perspective, in that not only did you do well in science but you also chose to study it at 'A' level, and then as a degree and are now pursuing it as a career. Using your own personal recollections to inform your current beliefs about the affective value of practical work for the pupils you teach fails to take account of the fact that, in all likelihood, the vast majority of your peer group at school did not find the same practical tasks exciting, interesting and/or fun and probably chose not to pursue science post compulsion.

Review

This chapter has suggested that what many teachers frequently refer to as 'motivation' and you might, at this point, want to reflect on your own use of the word, is, in a strict psychological sense, better understood as non-enduring situational interest. The fact that situational interest, unlike personal interest or motivation, is unlikely to persist beyond the end of a particular practical lesson helps to explain why pupils' need to be continuously re-stimulated by the frequent use of practical work. Once this fact is recognized the reason why many of those pupils who claim to like practical work also claim to have little, if any, personal interest in science, or any intention of pursuing it post compulsion, becomes clearer. For while these pupils *do* like practical work their reasons for doing so appear to be (Table 2.1) primarily that they see it as *preferable* to non-practical teaching techniques that they associate in particular with more writing (Edwards and Power, 1990; Gardner and Gauld, 1990; Hodson, 1990; Denney and Chennell, 1986; Hofstein and Lunetta, 1982). However, what has also been shown (Table 2.4) is that the proportion of pupils, within each Year group, who claim to like practical work in its own right, as against simply preferring it to writing, decreases as the pupils progress through the school. One contributory factor to this is that pupils are, during visits to the school in Year 6, presented with an artificial image of school science, in which science and practical work are essentially one and the same and that practical work has, as its key features, 'fun', 'excitement' and 'enjoyment'. Yet, it would seem, from the pupils' comments, that within their first year at secondary school, during which time the novelty of being in a laboratory environment appears to wear off, they become disillusioned by the fact that the *reality* of school science is very different from the image that we, as teachers, initially seek to create in order to make our subject appear attractive.

Finally, we have considered the affective value of practical work as a means of contributing towards effective behaviour management. In this respect I have suggested that when faced with having to teach science to pupils, and this is particularly so at Key Stage 4, who have little, if any, interest in science, or in some cases of even being in the lesson, practical work provides an effective 'coping' strategy. While accepting that it might be unlikely that these pupils would learn any more from practical, than from non-practical, work the use of practical work can make them easier to deal with from a behavioural perspective. While this might be considered as a 'lost' learning opportunity, it is arguable that among those pupils who have already 'switched off' the use of practical work might mean that their perception of science will be less negative than it might otherwise have been were they compelled to undertake more demanding, non-practical, work.

Key Issues for Practical Work

Introduction

Much of the time spent planning practical work involves thinking about how to get pupils to do and observe things with objects and materials rather than thinking about how the pupils are to think about and learn from their actions and observation. This chapter considers the effectiveness of practical activities in school science – the key issues that need to be considered in order to maximize that effectiveness – and suggests that there is a need for a greater emphasis on a 'minds-on' approach to practical work.

As we have seen in Chapter 2, Donnelly (1998) suggests that one of the reasons for the frequent use of practical activities in science lessons is that many science teachers see its regular use as an essential part of what it *means* to be 'a science teacher'. That practical work 'seems the "natural" and "right" thing to do' (Millar, 2002 p. 53) means that for many teachers its use has become the basic modus operandi for the teaching of science. While this, in itself, is not necessarily a problem it does carry with it an inherent risk that its use can become so taken for granted that teachers cease to critically consider whether its use is always the most effective means of achieving the learning outcomes they want. Indeed your own experience in school, as well as research (Abrahams and Millar, 2008), probably means that you are already aware that frequently pupils do not learn the things you might want them to learn from a practical task. In addition many pupils can, over the medium to long term, only recall specific surface details of a practical task and are unclear as to why they undertook it or what they learned from it.

> Researcher: What other practicals do you remember?
> RL9: Well can you [addressing pupil RL7] remember that experiment that we had to do with a brick outside?
> Researcher: Was that with Mr Rainton?
> RL9: Yeah.
> Researcher: What do you remember?
> RL9: A big bang and all that.
> Researcher: And why did you do this practical?
> RL9: [Shakes head in the negative to indicate that they do not know].
> RL7: We don't know why, do we [addressing RL9]? We just liked doing it.

Issues like the one above have raised doubts in the minds of some science educators as to the real value of practical work within the context of science education. Osborne (1998) claims that practical work 'only has a strictly limited role to play in learning science and that much of it is of little educational value' (p. 156). Hodson (1991), in a similar vein, claims that, 'as practised in many countries, it is ill-conceived, confused and unproductive' (p. 176). Hodson's claim is not, I would suggest, an indictment of practical work per se but of practical work 'as practised'. Indeed very few of us would, I imagine, question the important role that practical work *can* play in science education. The question is not whether or not we should be using practical work or, as Osborne (1998) suggests, be restricting its use to a much more limited role, but rather how we can make its use more effective. To answer this question I want firstly to consider what we mean by 'effectiveness' and how we might measure it.

Effectiveness

In order to think about the effectiveness of a practical task it is useful to consider the stages in both developing such a task as well as in monitoring what happens when it is used. To do this I will use a model of the processes involved in designing and evaluating a practical task, developed by Millar et al. (1999 p. 37), and this can be seen in Figure 3.1.

Given that the aim of this model is to provide a framework for considering the effectiveness of a specific task *relative* to the aims and intentions of the teacher, the starting point (Box A) is an evaluation of the teacher's learning objectives in terms of what it is they want the pupils to learn. After the teacher has decided what they want the pupils to learn the next stage in the model (Box B) is for them to design a specific practical task (or use an existing one from a scheme of work) that has, or so they believe, the potential to enable the pupils to achieve the desired learning objectives.

However, because the pupils might not do exactly what the teacher intended them to do when the the task was designed, the next stage (Box C) considers what the pupils actually do when they undertake the task. There are various reasons as to why the pupils might not do exactly what their teacher intended. For example, they might not have understood the instructions or, even assuming that they had and followed them meticulously, the apparatus itself might have been faulty. Yet even if the task is carried out according to the

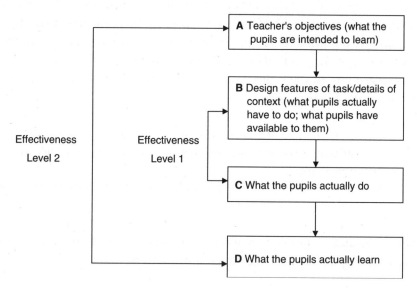

Figure 3.1 A model of the process of design and evaluation of a practical task (adapted from Millar et al., 1999, p.37)

teacher's plan, and all of the apparatus functions as it should, the pupils might still not think about the task using the ideas that the teacher had intended them to use. The last stage in the model (Box D) is therefore concerned with the question of what it is that the pupils actually learn as a result of their having undertaken the task.

Using this model enables the effectiveness of a specific practical task to be considered on two separate levels. The first level of effectiveness is concerned with what pupils *do* relative to what their teacher intended them to do. This level of effectiveness, referred to as 'level 1 effectiveness', is about the relationship between boxes B and C in the model mentioned earlier. The second level of effectiveness relates to what the pupils *learn* relative to what their teacher intended them to learn. This second level of effectiveness, referred to as 'level 2 effectiveness', is about the relationship between boxes A and D. This model enables questions about the 'effectiveness' of a specific practical task to be considered in terms of:

- Does the task enable the pupils to do the things the teacher actually wanted them to do when they chose to use that specific practical task?
- Does the task enable the pupils to learn what the teacher actually wanted them to learn when they chose to use that specific practical task?

Using this theoretical model of effectiveness in conjunction with Tiberghien's (2000) model of knowledge, in which there are two distinct domains: the domain of observable objects and events (o) and the domain of ideas (i), makes it possible to consider each of the two levels of effectiveness in terms of these two distinct domains. We are then in a position to analyse and discuss the effectiveness of any practical task in terms of two levels, with each level being sub-divided into two domains. In terms of task effectiveness these levels are defined in the following way:

- A task is effective at level 1:o if the pupils *do* with the objects and/or materials the things that the teacher intended them to do and, as a consequence, they see the intended outcome.
- A task is effective at level 1:i if the pupils *think* about the task using the ideas that the teacher intended them to use.

At level 2:o and 2:i the question of task effectiveness relates to whether or not it enables the pupils to *learn* the things intended by the teacher.

- At level 2:o a task is effective if the pupils *learn* and can recollect details about the objects/materials/events that they have observed and/or handled.

- At level 2:i a task is effective if the pupils *learn* and can recollect the scientific ideas that provide an explanation about the objects/materials/events that they have observed and/or handled.

A task is effective	. . . in the domain of observables (Domain o)	. . . in the domain of ideas (Domain i)
. . . at level 1 (what pupils do)	. . . if pupils set up and operate the equipment so as to see what the teacher intended.	. . . if pupils think about the task using the ideas intended by the teacher.
. . . at level 2 (what pupils learn)	. . . if pupils are later able to show how to set up and operate similar equipment.	. . . if pupils are later able to show understanding of the ideas they were meant to use in carrying out the activity.

Figure 3.2 A 2x2 effectiveness matrix

These two levels of effectiveness, each of which can be considered with respect to the two distinct domains of knowledge, can be represented (Figure 3.2) using a 2x2 effectiveness matrix.

If, as has been suggested (Millar et al., 1999; Solomon, 1988; Woolnough and Allsop, 1985), a central function of practical work is to provide a link between the domain of observable objects and/or events and the domain of ideas then effectiveness at level 2:i will be a necessary requirement. However if a task can, as arguably appears to be the case, only be effective at level 2:i if it is also effective at both level 1:o and 1:i then it follows that task effectiveness across level 1 is a necessary requirement if a successful link between the two distinct domains of knowledge is to be created.

'Doing' with objects and materials

Although Wallace (1996) has found that closed 'recipe' style tasks are unlikely to be perceived as either meaningful or engaging, and Arons (1993) reports that they are often considered to be dull and demoralizing, many teachers still chose to use practical tasks that are at, or close to, the closed 'recipe' end of the continuum (Abrahams and Millar, 2008). Although expressing a preference for open-ended investigations many teachers nevertheless appear to see the effective generation of a particular phenomenon, and/or set of results, by the majority of their pupils within the lesson as being of primary importance.

> Mr Normanby: Often the practicals are designed to be pupil friendly. You know, to make sure that within your double they'll see, at least most of them will, what you want.

In this respect we can think of the use of closed 'recipe' style tasks as a very successful means (Abrahams and Millar, 2008) of enabling most pupils, irrespective of academic ability, to set up and produce a particular phenomenon and analyse the results.

'Doing' with ideas

As Millar et al. (1999) have pointed out practical tasks 'do not [or at least should not] only involve observation and/or manipulation of objects and materials. They also involve the pupils in using, applying, and perhaps extending their ideas' (p. 44). While it is fairly self-evident as to what 'doing' with objects and materials means, 'doing' with ideas probably needs some clarification. The theoretical 2 x 2 matrix representation of practical work distinguishes, as we have seen, in the horizontal dimension between *doing* and *learning* and in vertical dimension between *observables* and *ideas*. 'Doing' with ideas can therefore be seen to refer to the process of 'thinking about' objects, materials and phenomena in terms of theoretical entities that are not themselves directly observable. If you have spent any time in the classroom you will be only too aware that, unfortunately, not all thinking necessarily means 'doing with ideas'. While the readings on a voltmeter can, for example, be thought about in terms of observables – the numbers on a dial or scale – it is when they are thought about in terms of their being a measure of the voltage – a non-observable property of batteries and other circuit components – that constitutes 'doing' with ideas.

It is important for you, as a teacher, to remember that the level 2 effectiveness of a practical task is a measure of what pupils do with ideas relative to what you the teacher intended them to do. A practical task can only have the *potential* to be effective (or ineffective) at level 2 if you actually intend that your pupils think about the observables using specific ideas.

Evidence for 'doing' with ideas

Before proceeding further it is important to recognize that because ideas, unlike objects and materials, cannot be observed, evidence of whether or not pupils use those ideas, has to be inferred mainly from what they say. In this respect what pupils say and how they say it is an indication not only of the ideas that the pupils are using to think about the task, but how those ideas are being presented to them by the teachers.

Since what pupils say is important in assessing whether or not they use the ideas intended by the teacher, their comments can usefully be assessed using a five-point scale. The scale ranges from lack of any appreciable use of scientific terminology (level i) to the full and coherent use of scientific terminology in discussing all aspects of the task (level v). In addition, the scale also distinguishes between talk that relates solely to observables (levels i–iii) and talk that also relates to doing with ideas (levels iv–v) (Table 3.1). It is however important to stress that while the use of scientific terminology provides a useful guide to

Table 3.1 Scientific terminologies: Different levels of use

Level i	Pupils do not use even basic scientific vocabulary but talk about all aspects of the task using colloquial terminology.	SH4: That purple colour sucks all the water, the water goes up, meets the black blobs, and it separates all the colours in the ink. KN10: We've got to identify which one's got Vaseline on and which one hasn't.
Level ii	Pupils use scientific vocabulary only to identify specific observables.	OD3: Can we have a heatproof mat? UF2: It's copper sulphate solution. UE2: It's iodine solution with starch.
Level iii	Pupils use scientific vocabulary only when talking about observables and procedures.	DE17: Copper sulphate and ammonia, well we didn't have the ammonia, so we just heated the copper sulphate. NK5: Like you've got a delivery tube which went down into a beaker which had a test-tube in.
Level iv	Pupils use scientific terminology when talking about observables and procedures and a mixture of scientific and colloquial terminology when talking about ideas	RN15: All the copper will get attracted to it 'cause it's negative, so it'll like it. FS12: The water's going to evaporate and the salt's going to be left behind. Researcher: Left behind? FS12: It's too heavy.
Level v	Pupils use scientific terminology when talking about all aspects of the task.	Researcher: What type of circuit is this? SK18: It's a series circuit. Researcher: So what's the voltmeter measuring? SK22: How much energy is going in and how much energy is coming out. Researcher: And what will that tell you? SK22: How much energy it has lost.

the ideas that the pupils might be using it does not mean that pupils who express themselves solely in terms of colloquial terminology are not thinking about the task. What it does mean is that those pupils are, for whatever reason, unfamiliar with the accepted scientific terminology.

This scale is therefore a useful way of allowing you to assess the extent to which you have been effective, as reflected in the language levels used by the pupils, in getting your pupils to do with ideas.

What has been found (Abrahams and Millar, 2008) is that there is a substantial difference between the effectiveness of practical work in the domain of observables compared to the domain of ideas. That is, although pupils are often successful in making the observations that their teacher intended they are unlikely to use/talk about the ideas intended by their teacher in a manner that would enable them to make sense of their actions and observations. One of the primary reasons for this is that many teachers appear (tacitly or explicitly) to still adhere to an inductive 'discovery based' view of learning whose underlying epistemological flaw, and the practical problems to which it leads, have long been recognized (see, for example, Driver, 1975). Yet the consequence for maintaining such a view is a belief that the ideas that the pupils are intended to learn about will simply 'emerge' of their own accord from the observations or measurements, just so long as the pupils produce them successfully.

This 'discovery based' view appears to me to ignore the fact that science is essentially an interplay between ideas and observations and, as such, an important role of practical work is to help pupils develop links between observations and ideas.

However, not only does the teacher need to introduce these ideas but, I believe, it would be advantageous for these ideas to be used by the pupils *during* the practical activity itself, rather than after the task has been completed (and possibly even in a subsequent lesson). Indeed the use of scientific ideas during the practical task, as pupils do things with objects and materials and make their observations, might help to facilitate the sort of 'envisionment' (Solomon, 1999) that better enables pupils to imagine what is going on 'beneath the observable surface'. Yet few practical lessons appear to be designed to stimulate such interplay between observations and ideas during the practical

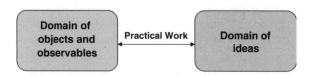

Figure 3.3 Practical work: Linking two domains of knowledge (adapted from Millar et al., 1999 p.40)

activity (Abrahams and Millar, 2008). While it is possible that some teachers might try to develop these links in subsequent lessons, the fact that the ideas are not available during the activity itself, when their use might help pupils understand the activity (to see its purpose) or their observations (to interpret these in the light of the theoretical framework of ideas), must reduce the effectiveness of the practical task as a learning activity.

In terms of implications for practice the suggestion here is that the two-domains model is a useful tool for enabling you to think about practical work. Firstly, it provides a means of assessing the 'learning demand' (Leach and Scott, 1995) of a particular task and recognizing there is a substantial difference in the learning demand of tasks in which the primary aim is simply for pupils to see an event or phenomenon or become able to manipulate a piece of equipment, and those tasks where the aim is for pupils to develop an understanding of certain theoretical ideas or models that might account for what is observed. Secondly, it draws your attention to the two domains of knowledge involved in practical work and the fact that one domain does not simply 'emerge' from the other. By being more aware of these issues and being better able to distinguish between tasks of relatively low learning demand and those where the learning demand is much higher, would then allow you to identify those tasks where pupils might require greater levels of support in order that what you intend them to learn might occur.

To do this it is necessary to ensure that the design of a specific practical task better reflects the fact that 'doing' things with objects, materials and phenomena will not lead to pupils 'learning' scientific ideas and concepts unless they are provided with a 'scaffold' (Wood et al., 1976 p. 90). The process of scaffolding provides the initial means by which pupils are helped to 'see' the phenomena in the same 'scientific way' that the you 'see' it (Ogborn et al., 1996). Indeed, Lunetta (1998) claims that 'laboratory inquiry alone is not sufficient . . . If pupils' understandings are to be changed towards those of accepted science, then intervention and negotiation with an authority, usually a teacher, is essential' (p. 252). One of the central issues is therefore the extent to which you acknowledge the need for this and build this into the design of the practical task.

However, given both the time constraints under which teachers operate and the clear importance that they associate with ensuring that most of their pupils successfully do with the objects and materials what is intended of them, 'recipe' style tasks are likely to continue to play a prominent role in science practical work. Yet if the extent of the cognitive challenge that pupils can sometimes face in linking their actions and observations to a scientific framework of ideas were better recognized, practical lesson time might be more equitably split between 'doing' and 'learning'. In so doing a greater proportion of the available time would be devoted to helping pupils use the ideas and concepts associated with the phenomenon that they produce, rather than simply seeing the production of the phenomenon as a successful end in itself.

Ensuring pupils do what you want

There are, as we have seen, various reasons why pupils might not do what you want them to do with objects and materials and I now want to consider these in more detail. In my own teaching experience these reasons – fire alarms, medical emergences and other such non-anticipated events aside – can be grouped together under four headings. These headings categorize, broadly speaking, the basic requirements that if not met, or only partially met, can prevent or at least hinder some, or all, of your pupils from doing what you intend. These four basic requirements are that:

(i) The pupils understand what they were required to do with the objects and materials provided.
(ii) The pupils are sufficiently proficient in the use of all of the required equipment to do what the teacher intended.
(iii) The equipment is in working order.
(iv) The phenomena are reasonably easy to generate.

While the overwhelming majority of teachers succeed in ensuring that the four requirements are met, I want to explore situations (all drawn from Abrahams, 2005) in which, as a consequence of one or more of the requirements either not having been met, or not having been met fully, some of the pupils were prevented, or at least hindered, from doing some or all of what their teachers had intended them to do with the objects and materials.

Understanding what is required to be done

In order that pupils are successfully able to do what the teacher intends it is vital that these intentions are communicated effectively to the pupils. To many teachers being effective in this respect means presenting the procedural instructions to their pupils using oral instructions in conjunction with *at least* one other presentational method. As an example the procedural instruction, given by Mr Overton, a biology teacher, whose Year 8 lesson was a physics activity designed to investigate the magnetic permeability of different materials, had three elements. Firstly, he provided and gave the pupils 2 minutes to read through a double-sided A4, commercially produced, worksheet that was part of the scheme of work (Smith, 2002) that he was following. Secondly, after the pupils had read the sheet and even though none of the pupils had any problem with reading, he called the class to attention and spent the next 3 minutes reading the entire worksheet out aloud to the class. Thirdly, having read the worksheet, he called the pupils around his bench where he spent another 5 minutes showing the pupils various pieces of equipment, including the materials to be tested, how to set the equipment up, as well as demonstrating how to carry out the actual testing procedure. While the last two methods of presentation, that occupied 8 minutes of the lesson, might have reinforced the information already presented in the worksheet neither contained any new information and given the limited time available the question of whether this is an effective use of lesson time is something that you need to consider for yourselves.

Another teacher, Ms Sharow, pointed out that while she had confidence that higher academic ability pupils would be able to follow just oral and/or written procedural instructions, she felt the need to supplement these two methods of presentation with a teacher demonstrations when teaching academically lower ability pupils:

Ms Sharow: Lower sets, I'll also do a demonstration, you know, 'this is how you set it up', 'plug this in here', 'plug that in there'. [Said very slowly to give an impression that she was explaining something to pupils who could only deal with limited and very basic information.] They find it very difficult to follow spoken or written instruction, they just can't concentrate.

In contrast Mr Dacre, who was concerned with the challenge of having to fit what he considered to be a relatively large practical task into a 55 minute lesson, chose to use only one presentational method in order to minimize the time spent on presentation and, as a consequence, maximize the time available for carrying out the task:

> Mr Dacre: I was concerned that the practical wouldn't be finished. I thought 55 [minutes] it was not an easy task for them to do in that length of time. In fact it works out at about 45 minutes because there has to be a bit of an introduction, you know where things are and what's going on, so we're talking about 40 to 45 minutes for six small practicals, it's not easy.

Having provided the pupils with two single-sided A4, commercially produced, worksheets, that were part of a scheme of work that he followed, Mr Dacre gave the pupils 4 minutes to read through the instructions. Then with the admonishment to 'Follow the instructions and you'll get the results that you need' he directed them to collect the apparatus.

Yet despite devoting a larger percentage (84%) of the total lesson time to task actualization than any other teacher within the study, none of his pupils managed to undertake all of the six tasks in the available time and a large proportion of the pupils still failed do what he intended them to do with some of the objects and materials.

What emerged from the observation of this, and other, tasks was that although the worksheets contained all of the procedural information needed to generate the desired phenomena, many pupils appeared unable (or in more cases were simply unwilling) to try to assimilate what was a relatively large amount of written procedural information within the short period of time prior to undertaking the task itself. Indeed when questioned on what they were actually doing, it became apparent that many pupils had not read the pro-cedural instructions:

> Researcher: What's this one?
> DE17: Copper sulphate and ammonia, well we didn't have the ammonia so we just used copper sulphate and it bubbled.
> DE18: 'cause sir's only brought the ammonia in now. [This was untrue; the ammonia had been on the front bench since the start of the lesson.]
> Researcher: Hang on, but number two [points to worksheet] doesn't say to heat it.
> DE17: What?
> DE18: Oh well.
> Researcher: Had you not read that?
> DE17: No.
> DE18: We just thought you had to heat them all.
>
>

> DE19: [Calling out loudly] Can I have a paper towel? [The liquid in the boiling tube had, on being vigorously heated, shot out over the desk.]
> Mr Dacre: Right come here you. Why did you heat that up? Which experiment is it, copper sulphate and ammonia? Right read out the sheet and tell me where it tells you to heat it.
> DE20: [The partner of DE19 looks at the worksheet.] It doesn't.
> Mr Dacre: Excuse me I'm asking him [points to DE19]. It says what?
> DE19: [Looking at worksheet.] It doesn't say heat it.

In findings similar to those reported by Berry et al. (1999), it transpired that the pupils, although initially reluctant to admit to not having read the instructions, did subsequently acknowledge that they had only skimmed through the worksheet, picking out those pieces of information, such as items of equipment or the names of materials, that were needed to enable them to start *doing* something:

> Researcher: So, have you read the instructions?
> DE2: Yar.
> Researcher: So you're filling all the test tubes up with sugar? [The instructions are to fill only one test tube with sugar.]
> DE2: Yar.
> DE3: [Reading the instruction sheet.] That's not right.
> DE2: Oh.
> Researcher: So have you read them [pointing to the instruction sheet], or haven't you?
> DE3: No.
> DE2: I have read them [laughs], but not very well.
>
> Researcher: So is it important that you read the instructions?
> DE18: Like we didn't [laughs and points to the equipment], we just checked what we needed to get.

The fact that the pupils just wanted to get on with 'doing' supports the claim made by Berry et al. (1999) that pupils often ignore instructions because they perceive a practical task solely as a 'hands on' physical activity and focus their attention only on what is necessary to enable them to engage with the 'doing' element of the task and this is something that you need to be aware of.

Indeed two teachers, whose tasks had been less effective in getting the pupils to do with the objects and materials what they had intended, attributed this lack of effectiveness to the pupils' failure to follow the procedural information rather than to any deficiency in the procedural information that they themselves had provided:

> Mr Dacre: I think one needs to plug away at the fact that sometimes we [the pupils] need to follow instructions so that we get the right answer.
>
> Researcher: Was that [task] successful?
> Mrs Ugthorpe: No, because lots of them didn't, they can't follow instructions.

While it is reasonable to assume that some pupils might be unwilling to engage with the instructions they are provided with, there are cases, particularly in practical work (Johnstone and Wham, 1982; Johnstone, 1980; Johnstone and Kellett, 1980), where rather than being unwilling the pupils are unable to do with the objects and materials what the teacher intended due to what Tamir (1991) refers to as 'cognitive overload' (p. 16). Cognitive overload can occur when too great a demand is placed upon pupils' working memory as a result of their having being presented with too much information too quickly (Johnstone and Wham, 1982). If the pupils' working memory does become overloaded, then not only is there a greater likelihood that they will be unable to fully understand what you want them to do but, as Delamont et al. (1988) have argued, it will be more difficult for them to adhere to the procedure so as to generate successfully the desired phenomenon. Presenting the procedural information on a 'need to know' or 'bite-size' basis, that is, only when it is required to undertake a particular aspect of a task, means that you are more likely to be successful in getting your pupils to do what you want them to do with the objects and materials.

A nice example of this approach can be seen with Mr Rainton, a chemistry teacher, teaching a Year 10, low academic ability class, the topic of electrolysis, who used material from a textbook as well as material he had designed himself. The task was composed of three separate sub-units, the first two of which, the electrolysis of hydrogen chloride (hydrochloric acid) and the electrolysis of copper sulphate solution, were taken from the textbook while the third, the electroplating of a five pence piece with copper, was his own design. The information for each sub-unit was presented using up to three presentational methods and only after each task had been undertaken and summarized did Mr Rainton move on to present the procedural information for the next sub-unit. Therefore while the *total* amount of procedural information remained unchanged, the effect of splitting it into smaller discrete packages was to reduce the demand being made on the pupils' working memory and, as a consequence, reduce the risk of cognitive overload with respect to each particular sub-unit.

Proficiency with the use of the equipment

Given that your pupils have understood what it is that you want them to do, the next requirement, if they are to successfully generate the desired phenomena and/or data, is that they (and of course you) be sufficiently proficient in the use of any of the relevant equipment. It is important to emphasize here that pupil proficiency with equipment is likely to vary, even within the same class and that familiarity with a piece of equipment, in the sense that it has been used before and might be recognized by the pupils, does not necessarily imply proficiency with its use. For example, while the actual construction of a basic series circuit containing a number of bulbs presented only minor problems for a few pupils taught by Ms Ferrensby and Mrs Duggleby, there was a widespread inability to obtain the current readings required to illustrate the conservation of current. There were a number of reasons for this, but all were indicative of a lack of proficiency with the use of an ammeter. When the reasons for this were examined it emerged that the most widespread problem was that the pupils did not understand that the polarity sign of the current, as indicated on an ammeter, was merely an indication of the direction in which the current was flowing and that it was the magnitude of the ammeter reading alone that measured the size of the current. However, a large proportion of pupils perceived any needle deflection to the left of the zero, when using analogue ammeters with a centre scale zero (CSZ), as being less than any deflection of the needle to the right of the zero, irrespective of its magnitude. For example, rather than perceiving a reading of 0.8 amps to the right of the zero (CSZ) and a reading of 0.8 amps to the left of the zero as being indicative of a conserved current that, because of reversed polarity connections, was flowing in the opposite direction, the pupils perceived the latter as being 1.6 amps less than the former, suggesting that the current had been consumed. Similarly pupils using digital ammeters perceived a current of 0.4 amps as being 0.8 amps more than a current of (minus) – 0.4 amps, rather than as a current of the same magnitude that differed only in its direction of flow. In the case of analogue ammeters, in which the zero was on the left of the scale (LSZ) and needle deflection could only occur in a clockwise manner, pupils perceived zero movement of the needle as being indicative of a broken ammeter (especially when they could see that current was flowing because a bulb in the circuit was on) rather than as an indication of incorrect polarity connections. Indeed from the comments made by the pupils, similar problems had also prevented some of them from obtaining results in previous practical tasks:

> FY3: Last week we couldn't get it to work.
>
> FY2: [Inserts a LSZ ammeter into circuit.] The ammeter wasn't working.
>
> Researcher: Is that reading anything, your ammeter, or not?
>
> FY3: No.
>
> FY2: No, we've got another one. [Replaces the first LSZ ammeter with another LSZ ammeter that also gives no reading. FY2 bangs the desk angrily with their hand.]
>
> Researcher: Why didn't the ammeter read anything?
>
> FY2: I don't know.
>
> FYa: Ours is also broken. [FYa has come over with a LSZ ammeter and makes this comment while pointing to the zero deflection on the ammeter being used by FY2 and FY3.]
>
> Researcher: Try again. [Pupils do and again obtain zero deflection.] So the lights are working but the ammeter isn't working. Is that what happened last week?
>
> FY2: Yes.
>
> FY3: Yeah.
>
> FY2: Yeah the ammeter isn't working.
>
> Researcher: Watch. I swap them around [the connections to the LSZ ammeter] and what happens?
>
> FY3: It works. [Really excited.]
>
> FY2: Thank you.
>
> Researcher: Hello. So you're working on your own?
>
> FY4: Yeah.
>
> Researcher: What have you found?
>
> FY4: That the ammeter isn't going up really.
>
> Researcher: Is it not?
>
> FY4: I don't know if it's not working. [Not only has the pupil connected the LSZ ammeter incorrectly but they have also connected both the a.c. and d.c. output sockets on the power pack to different parts of their circuit.].

The consequence, as the following example illustrates, for what pupils learn (or fail to learn), that can arise from a lack of proficiency with a basic item of equipment can be appreciable:

Researcher: What did you find?

DY5: We found it went there [points to the right of zero on their CSZ ammeter] now it's gone there. [Points to the needle that is now on the left of the zero.]

DY6: So it's gone down.

DY5: So it went more and then less [points with finger to indicate the flow of an electric current into and out of the bulb] so our prediction was right.

Researcher: Your prediction was right. Are you happy?

DY5: Yes.

DY6: Yeah.

Researcher: So you think you've found what you predicted? Now what happens if I do this? [Switches ammeter polarity so as to change the direction of needle deflection from the left of the zero to the right.]

DY5: Oh. [Said in a long drawn out manner.]

Researcher: Now what's happened?

DY5: It's where it was before. [Clear surprise in their voice.]

DY6: I know but have you done both ways? (sic) [DY6 who had connected up the circuit in this group was unhappy at the alteration that the researcher had made and so reverses the polarity of the ammeter connection in order to restore the left of zero needle reading.]

DY5:It's gone up and then it's gone down.

DY6: So we've [strong emphasis on 'we've'] connected these up.

DY5: It doesn't matter which we done. (sic)

Researcher: So what has your practical showed you then?

DY6: We found that it goes up more before and then it goes down after so it uses quite a lot of current.

DY7: Yeah.

In addition to the problem of connecting the ammeter correctly with regard to polarity, a number of pupils also lacked the basic skill required to read it with sufficient accuracy to enable then to ascertain that the current had the same value at all points within the circuit:

FY9: It's reading the same as last time which is eight.

Researcher: How many?

FY8: That's nought point something.

Researcher: Nought point something?

⇨

> FY8: Yeah.
> Researcher: Nought point what?
> FY8: Nought point two.
> Researcher: [To FY9.] What do you think it reads?
> FY9: There's one, there's five.
> FY8: [Interrupting] It's nought point two.
> Researcher: [To FY9.] What do you think it is?
> FY9: [Shrugs to indicate that they do not know.].

Asked about this lack of proficiency, Ms Ferrensby claimed that the pupils had been explicitly taught how to use an ammeter through the use of both a worksheet and a teacher demonstration:

> Mrs Ferrensby: Right the first lesson last week I showed them how to use an amme-ter. They actually had a worksheet first of all which had various dials on and had a go at reading from them and then, that is when I had them around the front, and I demonstrated how to set it up . . . . I did show them, I didn't assume that they knew, I showed them exactly because an ammeter is a new word for them, a new concept, so I talked about ammeters in the lesson before this one.

While there can be little doubt that pupils do need to be taught new practical techniques (Millar, 1991), such as measuring current with an ammeter to within 0.1 amps or using a millimetre scale, there is also a recognition (White, 1996) that improved proficiency with such techniques can only come about with actual repeated practice. It has been suggested (Masters and Nott, 1998) that if children are to become proficient practitioners they 'need to be explicitly taught *and then* they need to practice so that techniques and tactics become implicitly known' (p. 214. Italics in original).

Furthermore, while pupils might be sufficiently proficient with the use of a CSZ analogue ammeter such proficiency is not necessarily directly transferable to either a LSZ, or digital, ammeter, a point borne out by the comments of one of the pupils:

> Researcher: [Points to analogue ammeter being used by the pupil.] Do you find these easy to read?
> FY9: The one I used last week [looks around the laboratory and points to a digital amme-ter on the next bench] was easy because it was a bit different but this one is hard.

While Ms Ferrensby was sufficiently proficient in the use of ammeters to be able to assist pupils who found them difficult to use, other teachers were less able to help their pupils because they too were not proficient with all of the equipment being used. For example, Dr Kepwick appeared, despite her research experience as a biochemist, to be unaware, and certainly did not inform the pupils, that the low voltage power pack being used, in addition to having an on/off switch that is illuminated whenever the device is turned on at the mains, has a re-settable fuse that can 'pop' out if too large a current is drawn. Yet with this type of power pack even if the fuse blows, preventing any current from passing through the circuit to which it is connected, the on/off switch remains illuminated as an indication that the device is still connected to the mains electricity supply. What became clear during the practical task was that none of the pupils, all of whom had used the device on numerous occasions over the previous two years, were aware of this fact. As a consequence of this there were pupils who continued to follow the procedural instructions through to the end unaware that, although the on/off switch was illuminated, the fuse had blown and so no electric current was flowing through their circuit. While Dr Kepwick made no mention of the need to monitor the power pack at all, Mr Ulleskelf, a chemistry teacher with considerable experience, actually drew the pupils attention *only* to the need to ' be very careful to make certain that the light [points to on/off switch] is on the lab pack' rather than of the need to monitor the fuse. The following discussion took place with two pupils who had spent most of the time allocated to doing the task using a power pack in which the researcher had observed that, as a consequence of the two electrodes touching soon after they had started to use it, the fuse had blown:

Researcher: What did you find?
UF14: They [the electrodes] stayed the same.
Researcher: They stayed the same?
UF15: Yes they did.
Researcher: Has that surprised you?
UF14: Yes.
UF15: Yes.
UF14: Because we thought one of them would have changed.
Researcher: Which one [points to the electrodes] did you think would change?
UF15: That one, [points to cathode] the cathode one I think
UF14: The cathode
Researcher: Would you want to do this practical again?
UF15: We did it in physics four weeks ago. [Both pupils laugh.]
Researcher: You've done the same practical, the same one?
UF15: Yeah.

> UF14: Yes.
> UF15: It worked that time.
> UF14: It worked then.

At this point UF15, examining the circuit closely, offers an explanation for the failure of the cathode to increase in mass:

> UF15: Maybe this, this [points in the general direction of the equipment] isn't working.

In response UF14, who was now also examining the equipment, refers to the fact that the on/off switch was, and continues to be, illuminated:

> UF14: [Points to the power pack light.] No, because the light is on.
> Researcher: Was the fuse in? [The fuse had 'popped' out, having blown previously, and needed resetting.] The light will stay on even if the fuse is out.
> UF14: Ah. [Apparently unaware of this fact.]
> UF15: Oh.

Similarly, despite the fact that Dr Kepwick moved from group to group – including groups in which the fuse had clearly blown – she seemed unaware of this problem. It became evident, when the pupils were questioned, that they had received no instruction in the basic use of the power packs:

> Researcher: Ah you've got no power. [The pair had attracted one paper clip with a coil having two turns and no paper clips with a coil having either ten or twenty turns.] Now this thing here [points to the fuse button] is called the fuse and when it pops out there's no electricity going through it. [Researcher resets fuse and, in so doing, the twenty turn coil attracts four paper clips lying near to it.]
> KK9: It works, it works.
> KK10: [Hops about excitedly].

Two pairs of pupils, who had just been visited by Dr Kepwick, were then questioned:

Researcher: Your fuse has also popped out [points to fuse]. Did you notice that your power pack's not working? Have you not used this power pack before?

KK17: We have, but no one's ever told us that before.

Researcher: [Points to the blown fuse on their power pack.] Do you know what that black button sticking out is on the power pack?

KK11: [Reading the label above the button.] Reset.

Researcher: It means it's not working. So how long have you been doing your experiment without knowing that the electricity wasn't going through the electromagnet?

KK12: That must have just happened.

Researcher: No it only happens when the power was on. [The power pack was now turned off.]

KK11: [Turns on power pack and points to the illuminated on/off switch.] See?

Researcher: No that light will be on even when that's [points to fuse button] out.

It also emerged that Mrs Kettlesing had introduced Dr Kepwick's Year 9 class to the use of the power pack during a lesson on making an electromagnets similar to the one observed in this study with Year 7 pupils. Yet in this study, when Mrs Kettlesing introduced her Year 7 pupils to the power pack for the first time, she made no mention about the fuse, its purpose, or how to re-set it. Indeed, in a manner reminiscent of Dr Kepwick's Year 9 class, the fact that the fuse had, unbeknown to some of the pupils, blown during the observation of the magnetic field generated by a coil with only a few turns meant that the larger coil, when subsequently tested, did not generate any magnetic field. This led some pupils to reject their initially correct hypothesis:

KG11: I thought the bigger one would work more.

Researcher: Why?

KG11: Because.

KG12: It's more…

KG11: Because you'd think it'd have more magnets, more magnetic, because it's bigger.

Researcher: So what have you learnt from this practical?

KG12: Little coils make better magnets out of electricity.

Even a very basic practical task, such as the one designed by Mrs Risplith, a biology teacher, to enable academically low ability Year 9 pupils to see that heart rate and pulse were the same, was ineffective because the pupils lacked sufficient proficiency with the use of a stethoscope and/or the technique to locate their own pulse that was needed to generate successfully the required data:

> Researcher: Did you manage to hear your heart beat with a stethoscope?
> RH6: Well ours certainly…
> RH7: [Interrupts.] No.
> RH6:…was certainly got bust (*sic*) we never heard no der-der-dum.
> Researcher: [Having checked that the stethoscope is working.] You didn't manage to hear it?
> RH6: Bloody waste of time.
>
> Researcher: What have you found?
> RH9: Nothing yet because I can't find my pulse. [The researcher demonstrates how to find a pulse.] Oh yeah.

The reason why pupils failed to produce the desired phenomenon was not that the use of stethoscope and/or the technique to locate their own pulse was an unduly difficult skill for the pupils to master. Indeed the researcher had found it relatively easy to teach the pupils how to do both. Rather the ineffectiveness of the task arose because Mrs Risplith had assumed that the use a stethoscope, a new and previously unused piece of equipment, and the location of a pulse, something that she did not ascertain that the pupils actually knew how to do, were so simple to use/do that specific instruction and practice were not needed before the pupils used both to generate the desired data.

In a similar manner Mrs Ugthorpe had also assumed that the use of chemical indicators to test for starch, protein and fat were so basic that, provided instructions were given to the pupils on how to use them, there was little need for any prior familiarity with their use. However, what was found was that the pupils' lack of familiarity with these indicators meant that what should have been a relatively quick and simple task, involving little more than common-sense, took an entire lesson in which many of the pupils failed not only to complete the tasks, but also to see the desired phenomena:

Researcher: So what have you got in there? [Points to a tray in which the pupils have been observed to mix iodine and starch solutions.] Explain to me.

UE3: We've got some iodine solution and some of that stuff. [Points to bottle of starch solution on the Mrs Ugthorpe's bench.]

Researcher: Iodine and starch [solutions] mixed together. Right so you've got a little tray of iodine and starch [already mixed together] and you're dripping that onto your bread.

UE4: Yeah.

UE3: Yeah.

Researcher: And what's that going to tell you?

UE4: I haven't got a clue.

Researcher: Right, what's in there?

UE6: It's two drops of iodine solution and the starch solution.

Researcher: So you've mixed the iodine and the starch solution and you've got this nice [points to tray with bluish/black solution] and now you're adding your chocolate to it. Is that what you're meant to do?

UE6: Yeah.

UE7: Yeah, that's what we were told to do. [Mrs Ugthorpe had given such instruction.].

Because the sole aim of the task used by Mrs Ugthorpe was for the pupils to produce and see the positive test results, the fact that the pupils lacked proficiency affected the overall effectiveness of the task in terms of getting the pupils to do what the teacher intended them to do with observables.

The unproblematic functioning of equipment

Even if the pupils are proficient in the use of the equipment they can still be hindered or prevented from doing what you want them to do if some of the equipment that they require for the task fail to function as they are designed to do. Here it must be stressed that such failure does not refer to any relatively small proportion of equipment that might, in any practical lesson, reasonably be expected either not to work or to malfunction. Indeed it might be expected that part of your role as a teacher (and in some cases, if you are fortunate, that of the laboratory technician) during a practical lesson is to repair or replace those items that do fail or malfunction. While equipment failure can occur in biology and chemistry lessons, for example yeast can fail to activate and burette taps can (and frequently do!) leak, it is in physics, with its dependency on a greater number of different pieces of apparatus, in which more failures might be anticipated, reflecting the well-known maxim that, 'if it looks horrid it's biology, if it smells horrid it's chemistry, but if it doesn't work it's got to be physics'. Generally speaking most of the equipment failures that you, as a science teacher, will encounter will relate to a relatively small number of basic pieces of apparatus such as bulbs, plotting compasses, ammeters, voltmeters and crocodile clips. While such failures are relatively common they tend only to involve a relatively small proportion of the equipment used and, in my own experience, such failure tends to favour electrical apparatus – a reflection probably of the fact that this type of equipment is less robust. While equipment failure can sometimes be frustrating for the pupils (and you) it tends only to slow pupils' progress rather than actually prevent them from successfully doing what you want them to do. Again, your best means of avoiding such pitfalls (although this is basic common sense) is to check, or ask your laboratory technician to check, the state of the equipment prior to the lesson and to have an adequate supply of replacement items ready to hand.

Phenomena and their ease of generation

However, even if your pupils understand what they are required to do *and* are sufficiently proficient in the use of the equipment *and* this all happens to be in working order, they may still fail to do what you want them to do unless the phenomena themselves are reasonably easy to generate or observe. Although it has been claimed (Hacking, 1983) that phenomena are inherently difficult to produce within the science research laboratory I would tentatively suggest that you are more likely to find this to be a problem in practical tasks at 'A' level. That said, I want to give you an insight into two tasks, in which the generation of the phenomena could be considered to be slightly problematic.

The first of these two slightly problematic tasks was taught by Mr Oldstead, a biology teacher, and required Year 8 pupils to heat a sample of a waxy material, contained in a boiling tube, in a water bath to a temperature above its melting point. Having melted, the wax was to be removed from the water bath and its temperature recorded every minute as it was allowed to cool to room temperature and, in so doing, re-solidify. The data collected was to be used to plot a change of state cooling curve, in which the teacher anticipated that a distinctive temperature plateau would be visible. While the plateau can emerge as little more than an inflection in the cooling curve it is possible to ensure a more pronounced plateau through a judicious choice of the amount of solid to be used. That is, the amount of material must be determined so that there is sufficient wax to prevent it from cooling too rapidly – a fact that results in little more than an inflection in the cooling curve – but not too much to prevent the liquid from completely solidifying within the time (approximately 60 minutes) allocated to a typical double lesson. This particular problem is, in the experience of the researcher, usually avoided by having a laboratory technician prepare the boiling tubes with the appropriate quantity of material before the lesson. Another problem that can occur is that the material can be heated to a temperature considerably above its melting point thereby extending the time required to cool and solidify beyond that available. However, the likelihood of this occurring can be reduced if the procedural information clearly states the temperature to which the material is to be heated before allowing it to start cooling, an approach used by Mr Oldstead:

> Mr Oldstead: Hopefully the temperature of the wax by the time you've heated it in pretty hot water will have reached about 70° or 80° . So just make sure it's 70° to 80° at the start. And then at the start of the experiment take it out. So just make sure it's 70° to 80° at the start.

It was not possible to assess the extent to which the pupils undertaking this task had been able to generate the desired cooling curve plateau. This was because, rather than instructing the pupils to plot the cooling curve as they collected the data, Mr Oldstead had instructed them to collect all of the data first and, since this took most of the lesson, there was insufficient time before the end of the lesson for them to plot the cooling curve. You might like to consider whether you think it appropriate to separate the graphical representation of the plateau from the practical task used to generate the data.

The second task, taught by Mr Ulleskelf, required the pupils to measure the change in the mass of the cathode and anode as a result of electrolysis. While the pupils can, if proficient with the use of a top-pan balance, measure the resultant changes in the mass of the cathode and anode, problems can occur. The copper, which is deposited on to the cathode, can flake off during electrolysis and/or be inadvertently wiped off if the pupils dry the cathode prior to placing it back on the balance. There is also the potential problem that the anode can break up during electrolysis, making it difficult for the pupils to ascertain the total mass that remains. These problems, if left unresolved, can make it problematic for the pupils to obtain readings that are accurate enough to show that the loss in mass of the anode is equal to the gain in mass of the cathode:

> Researcher: What did you find?
> UF16: Got heavier.
> Researcher: Which one?
> UF16: Both of them.
> Researcher: Both of them?
> UF17: We think our results are a little bit wrong.
> Researcher: Why?
> UF17: Because we don't think they're meant to both, to gain the same amount.
>
> Researcher: What did you find?
> UF10: I don't know. [Points to bottom of beaker.]
> Researcher: Oh, it's at the bottom, [points to anode that has broken up and is now in pieces at the bottom of the beaker], so you haven't reweighed it?
> UF10: No, not yet.
> UF11: The problem is we can't reweigh it because that thing's snapped.

However, the likelihood of these problems occurring can be reduced if the procedural instructions stipulate clearly, as did those provided by Mr Rainton who undertook a similar, although not identical, task, that the supply voltage needed to be relatively low, the electrodes were not to be disturbed during the electrolysis process and that the drying of the electrodes was to be undertaken with great care:

> Mr Rainton: To work properly you've got to reduce the voltage so put it down to two volts . . . . you've not got to move it, so once it's set up I want you to leave it there . . . Just put it onto the paper towel and just dry it a little bit, don't do anything else. Put it onto the paper towel, just dry it a little bit, don't [the word is strongly emphasized] rub it just leave it on the paper towel.

Both these tasks, while slightly more challenging than the others within the study, can, if the pupils are provided with sufficient procedural information, be used successfully to generate a desired phenomenon. Indeed, were they not a relatively reliable means of generating particular phenomena, it is highly likely that teachers would, long ago, have ceased to use them.

Finally you might find it reassuring to know that if a practical task repeatedly fails to work as you intend you would not be the first to consider 'desperate' measures to ensure that the 'right' results are produced the next time you try it. Nott and Wellington (1997 p. 396) discuss 'conjuring', in which teachers fraudulently produce the desired results, and 'rigging' (ibid.), in which the adjustment of the variables is made surreptitiously: 'we have heard of teachers doping water with sodium bicarbonate and/or using "grow lights" in photosynthesis experiments so that oxygen is reliably yielded' (p. 396).

While meeting these four basic requirements does not guarantee an effective lesson, a failure to meet one or more of them is likely to mean that your lesson will not be as effective in meeting your learning objects as you might have hoped. In the next chapter I want to look at how one teacher succeeded in his lesson effective at levels 1 and 2 and across both domains.

4 What Pupils Learn about Objects, Materials and Ideas

Chapter Outline

Introduction

The aim of this chapter is to consider practical work in terms of its effectiveness in getting pupils to learn what you want them to learn about both observables and the scientific ideas used to understand them. This form of effectiveness, which I have referred to as 'level 2 effectiveness' relates, as we have seen, to the relationship between your objectives – what you want the pupils to learn – and what the pupils actually learn, that is the relationship between boxes A and D (Figure 3.1).

Intended learning outcomes (learning objectives)

Before proceeding it is important to clarify what learning in each of the two domains of knowledge actually entails. The theoretical 2 x 2 matrix representation of practical work, which we saw in Chapter 3 (Figure 3.2), distinguishes in the vertical dimension between *observables* and *ideas* and in the horizontal dimension between *doing* and *learning*. The two lower quadrants, in the central column of the matrix, refer solely to objects and properties that can all be directly measured or observed. In this respect learning in the domain of observables refers to an understanding about objects, materials, phenomena, and the relationships between them, that are expressible *only* in terms of their observable properties. Conversely, the two lower quadrants on the right hand side of the matrix refer solely to ideas, none of which can be directly observed or measured. As such, learning and understanding in this domain is expressible *only* in terms of currently accepted scientific ideas, and the relationships between them, where the term 'ideas' includes concepts, theories and models.

This distinction, between learning about observables, and learning about ideas, becomes clearer when considered within the context of your possible learning outcomes (learning objectives). Table 4.1 shows possible learning objectives as well as the domain(s) to which they relate.

While these learning objectives are, for the most part, self-explanatory some of them need to be clarified before proceeding further. In this respect, in the second learning objective, a 'fact' is what Feyerabend (cited in Maxwell, 1962) refers to as:

> [A] singular, nonanalytic sentence such that a reliable, reasonably sophisticated language user can very quickly decide whether to assert or deny it when he is reporting on an occurrent situation. (p. 13)

In other words, as Millar (2004) succinctly states, a 'fact' is 'an observation statement that can be readily agreed, and is expressed in everyday language' (p. 9). Examples of 'facts' are that liquids take up the shape of the bottom of their container, and that water expands on freezing.

Table 4.1 Categorization of possible intended learning outcomes (learning objectives) and the domains to which they relate (adapted from Millar et al., 1999)

Intended learning objective	Domain
1. Identify observables and become familiar with them	Observables
2. Learn a fact	Observables
3. Learn how to use and/or set up equipment	Observables
4. Learn how to carry out a standard procedure	Observables
5. Learn a relationship	Observables/Ideas
6. Learn a concept	Ideas
7. Learn a theory/model	Ideas

In the fifth learning objective the term, 'to learn a relationship', relates to learning objectives that can exist in both the domain of observables and the domain of ideas. It is important here to point out that this is, in itself, not a controversial claim but simply one that recognizes that a particular practical task can provide the opportunity for learning about relationships to occur in two domains rather than just one. In the domain of observables this relationship refers to learning about the connection between objects, materials and phenomena in terms of their directly *observable* properties while in the domain of ideas it refers to learning about the connection between theoretical entities that are themselves not directly observable. That a practical task can provide learning opportunities with regard to relationships in both domains can be illustrated by reference to a simple practical task designed to investigate Hooke's law. In the domain of observables this practical task, in which one end of a spring is suspended from fixed point while weights are attached to the other, provides an opportunity for the pupils to learn about the relationship between the length of that *specific* spring, as it is measured with a ruler, and the weights that are suspended from its free end. In terms of learning in the domain of ideas the same practical task also provides the opportunity for the pupils to learn about the relationship between the applied force and the extension – both of which are continuous variables and are applicable to *all* springs – and which, within a certain range, produce a relationship known as Hooke's law. While recognizing that there can be grey areas between a relationship between observables and one between ideas I think that this distinction provides a useful means of enabling you to focus in on what it is that you want your pupils to learn.

Objective 7 refers to learning that is intended to develop the pupils' conceptual understanding of a model or theory. This would include, for example, understanding the attraction of a piece of paper to a rubbed polythene rod in terms of the negatively charged polythene rod repelling electrons in the paper thereby forming a local area of positive charge that, because unlike charges attract, is attracted to the rod.

While I think it important that you consider the effectiveness of each practical task you use (if not how will you know whether a particular practical task is effective in achieving your learning objectives and should, as such, be used again?) it is clear that many practical tasks are embedded within extended sequences of lessons in which you might make use of a variety of teaching strategies. Because of this you might decide to place a greater emphasis on the use of practical tasks in order to achieve those learning objectives that depend primarily on your pupils' observation of objects, materials, phenomena and procedures (objectives 1 – 4 and, when it relates to the domain of observables, objective 5) rather than on the development of their conceptual understanding. This is not to say that you might not also use practical tasks with the intention of developing your pupils' scientific knowledge (objectives 6, 7 and, when it relates to the domain of ideas, objective 5), although many science educators (Lazarowitz and Tamir, 1994; Hodson, 1991; Mulopo and Fowler, 1987; Hofstein and Lunetta, 1982; Blosser, 1981; Bates, 1978) have questioned its effectiveness to do so. Rather, it suggests that these latter objectives are more likely to be met through the use of a combination of teaching strategies in which practical tasks contribute towards, or help in (Millar, 2004), the development of conceptual understanding. Indeed it might be, as White (1979) has suggested, that the potential value of a practical task, as you see it, is that it provides an effective anchor: a 'memorable event' (p. 385) onto which scientific ideas, possibly learnt through other teaching strategies, can, by association, be recollected.

Assessing what pupils learn

The evaluation of the effectiveness of practical work for learning needs, as does *doing* with ideas, to be based on an analysis of what pupils say during, or immediately after, the completion of a practical task. While this approach does not provide any direct evidence for what the pupils will, at any subsequent time, be able to recollect it does provide what is arguably an upper limit as to what they are likely to be able to recollect in the future. This is because whatever pupils are able to say, or recollect, about a particular task is likely to be at its clearest and most detailed during, or immediately after, undertaking the task when everything is still fresh in their minds. Therefore if there is little evidence in the short term for your pupils having learnt what your intended, and by having 'learnt' what is actually being assessed is their ability to 'recollect', then it is unlikely that their recollections about that task will, at a later date, be any clearer or more detailed. Indeed it is arguably very likely that they will be less so, as Brooks and Brooks (1993) have pointed out, that teachers 'everywhere lament how quickly students forget and how little of what they initially remembered they retain over time' (p. 39). You should also think about the fact that although what pupils are able to recollect, without you prompting them, is not necessarily the same as what they have learnt (which might optimistically be substantially more), what they are able to recollect unprompted is *all* that they are *aware* of having learnt.

Pupil recollections

A frequent claim that I have found to be made by many pupils, similar claims have also been reported by Denny and Chennell (1986), and one with which you might also be familiar from your time teaching science, is that practical tasks help them remember. However, when these claims are investigated further it was found (Abrahams, 2005) that for many pupils practical tasks were in fact not at all easy to recollect and many of the pupils found, as has also been reported by Berry et al. (1999), task recollection to be relatively difficult. Yet although some pupils were initially unable to recollect any practical tasks they had done in the past, and some claimed (erroneously according to their teachers!) not to have done any practical work for over a year, it was found that they were often able to recollect a particular task after having their memory 'jogged' by the comments made by other pupils. The following extracts are examples of this:

Researcher: Can you remember any other practicals that you've done? [Pupils shake their heads to indicate no.] Even in Year 7?

DE9: Oh yes we did this, made this, cell bag thing.

DE10: Oh yeah [nodding head to indicate that they too now remember] with wallpaper paste.

Researcher: Can you remember any practicals you've done this year? [No response.] Or last year?

DX4: Oh, I remember, we did these like bridges.

DX5: Oh yeah. [Nodding in agreement.]

DX4: We had to make bridges out of bits of wood. We wanted this car to . . .

DX5: [Interrupting.] Yeah it was a kind of suspension bridge and we had to get this car over.

DX4: One sheet of paper and see if it would hold the car.

One pupil who was unable to recollect any specific practical tasks when asked to do so explained that this was because they needed something, in the example below this was a question, to act as a 'trigger' for their recollections:

Researcher: What other practical do you remember?

RN11: I don't really know, it's just that when you get a question it comes back.

In fact what it appears the pupils were actually claiming was not that they found *all* practical tasks easy to recollect but rather that they found *some* tasks – and then only a relatively small number – *easier* to recollect than *lots* of material taught using certain, although not all, non-practical teaching strategies:

> UF5: It's much better than doing it without no experiment because you're doing it like and you'll remember it more.
>
> NK9: Because that way [teacher-demonstration] you wouldn't remember as much because it wasn't you that did it.
>
> UF8: It's better to do things practically because then I've actually seen it work, I'll remember it, instead of just being told.
>
> OD4: You'll remember the experiment more than a piece of paper.

Yet the possibility that such claims were simply part of the rhetoric surrounding practical work is exemplified by one of the pupils who, having claimed to recollect more by being allowed to actually undertake a practical task, was, when asked, unable to recollect anything about any practical task that she had undertaken. Evidently realizing that this inability to recollect anything about previous practical tasks was inconsistent with her previous claim the pupil (OD4) offered the following by way of an explanation: 'Ok, you might not remember it more, but it's less boring than just writing stuff down'. Indeed, many of the claims made by the pupils about practical work, as we saw in Chapter 2, involved statements of *relative* preference in which practical lessons, possibly because of the frequent use of worksheets, were frequently seen as a preferable option because they provided an opportunity to avoid the need for too much writing.

Pupils were not however alone in claiming that practical tasks were easier to recollect than alternative teaching methods. In findings similar to those reported in two large-scale national survey studies into the nature and purpose of practical work in science education (Thompson, 1975; Beatty, 1980) I also found that some of the teachers – and you might like to consider if this applies equally to you – believed that practical tasks, especially when they generated the 'correct' results, provided an effective way of helping pupils to recollect facts and ideas:

Mr Saltmarsh: I think if things have gone well, in a specific practical, it does help the children to understand and remember what they've done, rather than just writing it down.

Dr Kepwick: I do feel, in my limited experience, that often practical will help them remember so much more than just being told or shown pictures or something like that.

Mr Oldstead: I think I believe strongly that by doing things you're more likely to remember it. I mean if I look at my own kids they're more likely to remember stuff and be able to do things if they have a go at it, they're practising and I believe the kids here are the same.

In terms of learning, previous research (Ward, 1956; Newbury, 1934) has found that teacher 'demonstration lesson is, of necessity, more definite in content than individual experiments. Thus, while it is effective for all pupils, it is particularly helpful to the weaker pupils' (Newbury, 1934 p. 99). Despite these findings many teachers, as the following examples illustrate, continue to believe that actually allowing academically weaker pupils to undertake practical tasks for themselves was especially helpful in enabling them to recollect information:

Mrs Kettlesing: I think the low ability [pupils] are more likely to remember it because they've done it themselves.

Mr Drax: I think that some [academically weak] pupils are helped to remember by doing it themselves.

Yet despite the claims of pupils and teachers alike many pupils, irrespective of their academic ability, find it difficult to recollect even three practical lessons from throughout their *entire* period of secondary education that, in some cases, can be almost five years – you might like to see how many your own pupils can recollect without you prompting them. In fact many pupils only appear able to recollect even this relatively small number of tasks if their memories are 'jogged' by comments made by other pupils or because the task that they are undertaking when they are questioned about practical work is similar to, and 'triggers' a recollection of, a task that they had previously undertaken. For example, while many of the pupils undertaking the chromatographic separation of dyes, with Miss Nunwick, recollected having previously undertaken a similar task, similar tasks involving chromatographic separation were not recollected by any other pupil in the study even though, and I ascertained this from the respective heads of department, it was carried out regularly in most of the schools within the study. Likewise pupils in Dr Kepwick's practical lesson, undertaking a task that involved electromagnets, were the only ones in the study who recollected having previously carried out a task that involved electromagnets even though it is highly probable that pupils in other schools would have undertaken similar tasks. Similarly it was only Mr Normanby's Year 11 pupils, observed undertaking a task that involved the refraction of light through glass blocks, who recollected undertaking the same task on a previous occasion even though, in my own experience, this is a commonly used practical task at Key Stage 3.

Even when pupils' memories were 'triggered', by the similarity between the observed task and a previous one, their recollections were vague and frequently involved little more than a recollection that they had set up the equipment and undertaken the task. The following extract, taken from an optics lesson involving ray boxes and lenses, is an example of just such a 'vague' recollection which might arguably have been expected given the relatively uninspiring nature of the practical task and the fact that it took place two or three years earlier:

Researcher: Have you undertaken this experiment before? [Mr Normanby had informed the researcher that the task had been undertaken by these pupils when in Year 8.]
NY5: No I don't think so.
NY6: Yeah we have, a couple of years ago.
Researcher: Do you remember what happened?
NY5: No not really no.
NY6: No I don't [pause] I remember setting it up, but I don't remember the exact lines [the observable ray paths].

Similarly, while the head of physics confirmed that most of the pupils in Dr Kepwick's class had carried out an identical task in Year 7 (Dr Kepwick was repeating the task as a means of revision for Year 9 SATs), most of those questioned had no recollection of having done so or, if they did, could recollect little more than the fact that they had undertaken something similar previously. The following examples, in which the pupils respond without any sign of hesitation or uncertainty, show the extent to which there was no recollection of their having previously undertaken the same task:

Researcher: Were your predictions based on your Year 7 results?
KK2: I haven't done it before.

Researcher: Have you done this task before?
KK4: No.
KK5: No.

Researcher: Have you done this before, in Year 7?
KK8: I don't think we've done this experiment before.
KK7: No.

Researcher: Have you done anything on electromagnetism before?
KK13: In Year 7, but I think I might have been away.
KK14: I might have been away also, I don't know.

Of two pupils questioned who did actually have some recollection of having carried out the task in Year 7, both felt that repeating the task provided an opportunity to go over/revise the material and, in so doing, it served to refresh their memories:

Researcher: You've done this before?
KK3: Yeah.
Researcher: So if it helps you remember, do you remember it from last time?
KK3: Yeah. When you do it once and then you do it again you sort of like remember it.
Researcher: Have you done this before?
KK1: Yeah I did it in Year 7.
Researcher: You've done the same thing?
KK1: Yeah.
Researcher: So is this going to help you?
KK1: Revision.

When questioned about what they thought they would remember about this task in six months time the pupils' responses did not coincide with the intended learning objectives stated by Dr Kepwick which were to determine the factors that affect the strength of an electromagnet. Instead the pupils believed that they would be able to remember the procedure used to demagnetize nails and paperclips that they, judging from the amount of laughter during the lesson, had found very amusing. This unplanned demagnetization incident, peripheral to the main task, had involved pupils climbing up onto their stools in order to drop magnetized nails on to the floor or, in some cases, placing them on the floor and stamping vigorously (in some cases overly so) on them so as to demagnetize them. In one particular case, that aroused a lot of laughter from those who witnessed it, one pupil, apparently trying to demagnetize their paperclips, threw a handful of them up into the air and allowed them to rain down onto the surrounding pupils, benches and floor:

> Researcher: If I was to come in half a year's time and ask you about this practical what do you think you'd remember?
> KK6: Paper clips. [Pupil gestures as if throwing something into the air and laughs.].
>
> Researcher: If I was to come back, in say half a year, what do you think you'd remember about this?
> KK12: I've learned that you have to drop the magnets [nails] to get the magnetic field out of it.
> KK11: Yeah I'll remember that bit. [Both pupils are laughing].

In this respect the findings appear to support a view expressed by one of the teachers in the study who, commenting on the extent to which he thought his Year 10 pupils undertaking a practical task would be able to recollect practical tasks on the same topic undertaken in Year 8, suggested that:

> Dr Starbeck: Most of the stuff will have faded. What I hope is when they do it in Year 10, although they'll have forgotten it, they'll go 'oh yeah, I remember that', and they'll get it faster the second time and, with a bit of luck, it might last a bit longer.

It is important to emphasize that what I am suggesting here is *not* that practical work is necessarily any less effective, in terms of what pupils recollect, than other teaching tactics – indeed it might even be more effective. Instead what I am suggesting, given the very limited descriptive nature pupil recollections about practical work, is that there appears to be little evidence to support the frequent claims made by teachers and pupils that practical work is an effective means of helping pupils recollect scientific ideas. Indeed Tables 4.2, 4.3 and 4.4 summarize, by subject, not only all of the tasks that the pupils were

Table 4.2 Details of biology tasks recollected by pupils

Pupil	Description of practical task	Pupil's recollections	Year when pupils claimed to have undertaken the task	Year when recollected
DE9	Making a model cell	That they did it and that it 'looked like sick'.	Year 7	Year 8
DE10	Making a model cell	That they did it.	Year 7	Year 8
SW6	Dissecting a pig's eye	That they nearly fainted.	Year 10	Year 11
RH7	Dissecting an egg	That it was hard-boiled. That they had to find a membrane.	Year 7	Year 9
RH6	Dissecting heart and lung	That they had to smash them because they were 'pulsing'.	Year 7	Year 9
DX2	Bread making	Getting a letter from a woman called Brown that asked them to investigate whether it was better to use room temperature or a proving oven for making bread. Making and eating the bread.	Year 6	Year 7
NK18	Energy in food	That they burnt popcorn. That they burnt sugar and saw it caramelize.	Year 8	Year 8
SH8	Bacteria	Putting samples of pond water and sterilized water onto a 'gel-thing' to see bacteria and 'stuff'. That bacteria are colonies.	Year 7	Year 8
SY11	Decay	Putting bread into bags and opening the bag at a later time and noticing a 'really bad smell'.	Unsure	Year 10
SY12	Diffusion	How the water, starch or 'something' can move through the wall of a potato chip and that some were soggy some were hard.	Unsure	Year 10
UF5	Enzymes	That they did it.	Unsure	Year 10
SY9	Conditions for starch production in green leaves	Putting the leaf on the tile with iodine and that it didn't produce the correct colours.	Year 9	Year 10
SW9	Testing reaction times dropping a ruler	That they did it on more than one occasion.	Years 6 and 7	Year 11

Table 4.3 Details of chemistry tasks recollected by pupils

Pupil	Description of practical task	Pupil's recollections	Year when pupils claimed to have undertaken the recollected task	Year when recollected
RH7	Evaporation	That it was 'amazing'.	Year 7	Year 9
DX4	Test for hydrogen	It gave a 'squeak'.	Year 7	Year 10
FY14	Test for hydrogen	A 'squeaky-pop' noise.	Year 7	Year 7
KD4	Separation of soil, salt and 'something else'	The procedure used. [However, the pupil could not provide any details of this.]	Year 7	Year 9
KD9	Separation of salt from salt water by evaporation	Seeing the salt	Year 6	Year 9
KD13	Separating things	There are different ways to separate things.	Year 8 and 9	Year 9
OD2	Making a match stick rocket	Wrapping the end of the match in silver-foil then lighting them and shooting them across the room.	Year 7	Year 8
KD12	Burning magnesium ribbon	The brightness.	Year 7	Year 9
OD4	Burning magnesium ribbon	It was 'spectacular'.	Year 7	Year 8
NK12	Burning magnesium ribbon in a crucible	The procedure. Watching it flare, a slight increase in mass.	Year 7	Year 8
SH8	Distillation	That it was a blue liquid and that they got water from it.	Year 8	Year 8
SH7	Distillation	They used a thermometer, a tripod and a Bunsen burner and hot water went through the tubes into a beaker.	Year 8	Year 8
DX1	Reactivity of group 1 metals	The teacher dropped it into the water.	Year 7	Year 10
DX2	Reactivity of group 1 metals	That they saw it.	Year 7	Year 10
NK13	Reactivity of group 1 metals	It exploded.	Year 7	Year 8
NK14	Reactivity of group 1 metals	We had a big tub of water and the teacher put potassium in the water and it went round and burst into flame. It looked 'impressive'.	Year 7	Year 8

(Continued)

Table 4.3 (Cont'd)

Pupil	Description of practical task	Pupil's recollections	Year when pupils claimed to have undertaken the recollected task	Year when recollected
RN8	Reactivity of group 1 metals	It was 'violent', it was potassium or phosphor.	Year 7	Year 10
RN9	Reactivity of group 1 metals	It was ox (*sic*) reaction, it reacts with oxygen.	Year 7	Year 10
SY5	Reactivity of group 1 metals	We had a big tub of water and the teacher put sodium or 'something' in the water and it 'whizzed' around.	Year 7	Year 10
DX4	Reactivity of group 1 metals	That they saw it.	Year 7	Year 10
NK4	Chromatographic separation of dyes	The procedure and the phenomenon.	Year 6, 7 and 8	Year 8
NK11	Chromatographic separation of dyes	That it was set up like a murder mystery.	Year 6, 7 and 8	Year 8
NK13	Chromatographic separation of dyes	That it was set up like a murder mystery.	Year 6, 7 and 8	Year 8
NK14	Chromatographic separation of dyes	That it was set up as if an unknown pupil had drawn with ink on another pupil's shirt.	Year 6, 7 and 8	Year 8
SH9	Heating oil	That they heated oil to 200°C and someone knocked it off the table and it spilt on the table and they had to move to another table.	Year 7	Year 8
UF17	Electrolysis	That they did it with a metal a few weeks ago.	Year 10 (Twice)	Year 10
UF15	Electrolysis	That they did it in physics four weeks ago.	Year 10 (Twice)	Year 10
UF4	Measuring gas	Collecting gas and measuring.	Year 10	Year 10
UF2	Measuring gas	Collecting gas over water to see how quickly 'it' reacts.	Year 10	Year 10
UF3	Measuring gas	Collecting gas over water to see which metal chips were more vigorous.	Year 10	Year 10
DE16	Using indicators	The colour scheme 'thing'.	Year 7	Year 8
FY11	Making indicator from red cabbage	How it was made.	Year 7	Year 7

(Continued)

Table 4.3 (Cont'd)

Pupil	Description of practical task	Pupil's recollections	Year when pupils claimed to have undertaken the recollected task	Year when recollected
FY14	Test for carbon dioxide	Used limewater.	Year 7	Year 7
DY22	Practicing to use a thermometer	Used a Bunsen burner and then recorded the temperature of the water as it cooled.	Year 7	Year 7
RN9	Flame tests	Iron filings sparkled in a flame.	Unsure	Year 10
FY10	Putting hydrocholic (sic) acid with vinegar	It fizzed.	Year 7	Year 7
RL7	Thermite reaction	There were sparks and it went 'bang'. There were iron filings in it because it made those little sparks.	Year 9	Year 10
RL8	Thermite reaction [demo]	It was powerful.	Year 9	Year 10
RL9	Thermite reaction	Used a brick, loud bang, sparks 'what was the most reactive', Lithium, iron filings making little sparks.	Year 9	Year 10
RN18	Thermite reaction	He used a brick and we had to go outside.	Year 9	Year 10
RN17	Thermite reaction	He put loads of different 'stuff' in it, set light to it and there was a 'loud whoosh'. It was 'exciting'.	Year 9	Year 10

Table 4.4 Details of physics tasks recollected by pupils

Pupil	Description of practical task	Pupil's recollections	Year when pupils claimed to have undertaken the task	Year when recollected
RH6	Compasses	A magnet always turns north.	Year 7	Year 9
SW9	Series circuits (drama with Dr Starbeck)	Walking on the tables.	Year 10	Year 11
SW8	Series circuits (drama with Dr Starbeck)	Walking on the tables pretending to be electrons.	Year 10	Year 11

(Continued)

Table 4.4 (Cont'd)

Pupil	Description of practical task	Pupil's recollections	Year when pupils claimed to have undertaken the task	Year when recollected
SW4	Series circuits (drama with Dr Starbeck)	Tables were wires.	Year 10	Year 11
SW5	Series circuits (drama with Dr Starbeck)	Tables were wires pupils pretended to be voltmeters.	Year 10	Year 11
NY6	Shone a light through a prism	That they did it.	Year 10	Year 11
DX4	Making a bridge	Using bits of wood and paper to make a bridge over which toy cars with weights could pass.	Year 6	Year 7
DX5	Making a bridge	That it was a suspension bridge.	Year 6	Year 7
SY4	Making a bridge	Using straws and paper to make a bridge over which toy cars with weights could pass.	Year 9	Year 10
SW1	Wiring a plug	That they did it.	Year 10	Year 11
KG5	Magnetic poles	Like repel, unlike attract.	Year 7	Year 7
KD3	Shone a light through a prism	That they did it.	Year 9	Year 9
SW11	'Car and weights'	That they did it to work something out.	Year 11	Year 11
UY5	Van de Graaff generator	It was static electricity.	Year 9	Year 11

able, when questioned, to recollect but also the very limited descriptive nature of their recollections about those tasks.

One of the findings to emerge from the data was that of the 68 recollections relating to practical tasks 60 per cent of them (41 recollections) related to practical tasks undertaken in chemistry while physics and biology accounted for only 21 per cent (14) and 19 per cent (13) of the recollections respectively. In all of the cases although the pupils were asked what practical tasks they recollected their recollections were in no way prompted by the researcher nor were they guided towards recollecting only those practical tasks that related to the same science subject as the practical task they were observed undertaking. However, what can also be seen (Tables 4.2, 4.3 and 4.4) is that even in those cases were the practical tasks were in a sense 'memorable' pupil recollections still tended to be very limited descriptive accounts of what they did with objects and materials and/or the phenomena that they observed. There was little, if any, clear reference in their recollections to the associated scientific ideas that would have enabled them to understand their observations.

An analysis of these recollections shows there to be, broadly speaking, two distinct types of task that pupils are able to recollect and that these can be categorized as being:

(i) Tasks about which the pupils can recollect some specific detail.
(ii) Tasks that pupils simply recollect 'having done' – and little else.

Those tasks about which the pupils were able to recollect specific details, rather than simply that they had a vague recollection of 'having done it', tended to be those that were, in some sense, unusual. Without attempting to rigorously define 'unusualness' it can be seen (Tables 4.2, 4.3 and 4.4) that, generally speaking, unusual tasks were those that exhibited one, or more, of the following three characteristics:

1. A distinctive visual/aural/olfactory component.
2. A 'gore' factor.
3. A novel context.

Of the 68 tasks recollected 27 (23 chemistry and 4 biology), or 40 per cent of the sample, were ones in which the pupils' primary, and in most cases only, recollection related to a distinctive visual/aural/olfactory component within the task. The 'gore' factor was evident in three of the most vividly recollected biology tasks, while in a further 18 (3 biology, 8 chemistry and 7 physics) the recollections involved tasks that were presented in what was, relatively speaking, an unusual context. Although it has been suggested (Gagné and White, 1978) that it is the act of undertaking a task, rather than merely reading about it or having it demonstrated, that makes its recollection more likely I would argue that the likelihood of task recollection depends, to a much greater extent, on the presence of at least one of the above three characteristics. Indeed like White (1979), who describes the visually spectacular ignition of carbon monoxide, that was *demonstrated* to him by his teacher, as an example of a practical task that he vividly recollects, many of the tasks recollected by the pupils in this study, in fact 21 per cent of them, were visually spectacular teacher demonstrations. Certainly in a subsequent discussion White (1996) describes memorable episodes as 'recollections of events in which the person took part *or at least observed.'* (p. 765. Italics added), a view that appears to acknowledge that it is what it is that is observed, and/or how it is presented, rather than necessarily who undertakes the tasks that determines whether or not the task becomes a memorable episode.

Learning about observables

What we have seen so far is that practical tasks are, generally speaking, very successful in getting pupils to do with the objects and materials what the teacher intended them to do in order to produce a particular phenomenon. Indeed in only a few cases, which were discussed in Chapter 3, were the pupils unable to produce the intended phenomena. It can be seen (Tables 4.2, 4.3 and 4.4) that what most of the pupils were able to recollect, and therefore what they themselves were aware of having learnt, related to what they had done (or observed their teacher doing) with observables. Yet while many had evidently learnt something about observables as a consequence of having undertaken a practical task, or having had it demonstrated to them, their recollections frequently involved little more than their being able to describe what they had done and/or seen. For example, Mr Dacre had used a practical task so as to get the pupils to learn about the directly observable signs of a chemical, as opposed to a physical, reaction yet, as he made clear after the lesson, the pupils had failed to make this distinction:

> Mr Dacre: Actual smoke comes out, not steam, or water vapour, but actual smoke. So it must be burning and I don't think anyone did [write it down]. So that's something we might go back to and revisit.

Contrast this with what one pupil (DE9) informed me that they had learnt, in Mr Dacre's lesson, from their observation of heating (vigorously) some sugar in a boiling tube which was, and this was also written on their work sheet, that the 'smell makes you feel sick'. It might therefore appear reasonable to assume that if a teacher wants, as Mr Dacre did in this case, for the 'pupils to "see" phenomena and experimental situations in particular ways; to learn to wear scientists' "conceptual spectacles"' (Driver et al., 1985 p. 193), a teacher would need to 'steer', or 'guide', them towards thinking about what they were doing and seeing in a particular way: in fact in the particular way that the teacher themselves sees it (Ogborn et al., 1996) using appropriate scientific ideas and/or models. In this particular task this would have required getting the pupils to 'see' the significance of the fact that it was smoke, an indicator of combustion and therefore chemical change, that was being given off rather than steam or water vapour. It might therefore have been anticipated, as Wickman and Östman (2001) have suggested, that the pupils would have been told 'what to observe and how to talk and act in relation to observations' (p. 468). Yet neither during his task presentation, which at only 4 minutes was the briefest of those observed, or in the worksheet that he provided, was any mention made of what the pupils should specifically be looking at or for. Indeed when the pupils were asked by the researcher about what signs of a chemical reaction they were expected to note, many, as the following examples illustrate, simply did not know:

> Researcher: Ok, so how would you know if a chemical reaction had occurred with this one? [Water and anhydrous copper sulphate]
> DE11: Look for the signs.
> Researcher: Ok, what are the signs?
> DE11: I don't know.
>
> Researcher: Ok, now on this one you've put sodium carbonate and ironchloride [pointing to, and reading from, the pupils' worksheet] 'it bubbled up and over the top'. So there's lots of bubbles but you've said it wasn't a chemical reaction
> DE18 [Addressing the researcher.] Why, is it a chemical reaction?
> Researcher: I don't know I'm not a chemist.
> DE18 [Addressing DE17.] Is it a chemical reaction?
> DE17: What?
> DE18: If it bubbles up and over the top.
> DE17: We're only supposed to . . . [Shrugs to indicate that they do not know.].

Yet without specific guidance to ensure that pupils think about what they are doing and seeing in a particular way, the fact that they are successful in producing the phenomenon does not, in itself, ensure that they will learn what you intend them to learn from undertaking the task. It can, for example, be seen that despite pupil (DE18) having successfully produced the desired phenomenon, and their recollection of having seen lots of bubbles, they did not know, because Mr Dacre had not steered them towards thinking along those lines, to associate an observation of bubbles with the production of a gas and so to see it as it being a sign of a chemical reaction. Instead what many of the pupils in this study appear to have learnt, at least in terms of what they were able to recollect, was what it was about a particular task that made it, in some sense at least, unusual. Many of the tasks recollected (Tables 4.2, 4.3 and 4.4) were sufficiently unusual, in the sense that they exhibited either a distinctive visual/aural/olfactory component, or a 'gore' factor, or a novel context or a combination of these, to avoid the criticism made by one pupil (SW6) who claimed 'I don't remember very many chemistry ones [practical lessons] because they all seem the same to me'. Certainly the Thermite reaction (Conoley and Hills, 1998), in terms of being 'unusual', provides both a striking visual and aural component and, in the example recollected below, also involved a novel context – not only out of the laboratory but also out of doors and, due to the very high temperature of the reaction, it was ignited on a brick that had to be carried out by one of the pupils specifically for this purpose. The task itself is designed to show that finely powdered aluminium, if mixed with powdered oxide of iron and ignited with burning magnesium ribbon, will, because it is a more reactive metal than iron, reduce the latter in a highly exothermic reaction. Yet what was found, among those pupils who recollected this task, was that their recollections focused only on the visually and aurally spectacular nature of the reaction itself and the fact that it was undertaken outside the laboratory on a brick:

> Researcher: What other practicals do you remember?
> RN18: That one with the brick that we did outside that was quite good.
> RN17: Yeah he put loads of different stuff in it, set light to it, and it just whoosh, that was pretty exciting.
>
> RL9: Well can you [addressing pupil RL7] remember that experiment that we had to do with a brick outside?
> Researcher: Was that with Mr Rainton?
> RL9: Yeah.
> Researcher: What do you remember?
> RL9: A big bang and all that.
>
> RL7: Yeah and sparks.
> Researcher: What did you learn from it?
> RL7: That it went bang.

Pupil recollections about the Thermite reaction exemplify a general finding that memorable episodes, rather than acting as an anchor for the associated scientific ideas as White (1979) has claimed, merely provide an anchor for a descriptive, non-scientific, account of the task in which the memorable event itself occurred. It is important to stress again that an inability on the part of the pupils to recollect anything other than a fragmentary description does not necessarily imply that they might not have learnt more than this from the task. What it does however indicate is that frequently what the pupils are *aware* of having learnt – that is, what they are able to recollect without assistance – differs markedly from what the teacher had intended them to learn (and hopefully recollect). In the following example, of a task that had been used by Miss Nunwick three weeks prior to the lesson that she was observed teaching, the pupils had been looking at observable differences between physical and chemical reactions. One of these reactions had involved the pupils heating sugar in a boiling tube in order to observe the changes that occurred. Miss Nunwick, when I questioned her about this later, pointed out that her intended learning objective had been for the pupils to see the burning of the sugar as a sign of an irreversible chemical reaction. However, what the pupil who recollected this task was aware of having learnt (arguably they might already have known this because of their use of the term 'caramelize') was that sugar, when heated, is caramelized and other than the fact that they burnt the sugar this was the only part of the task that they claimed to be able to recollect:

Researcher: What practical do you remember?
NK18: Burning sugar.
Researcher: What did that show?
NK18: Nothing.
Researcher: Nothing?
NK18: It went caramelized.
Researcher: But what was it meant to show you?
NK18: I don't know, I can't remember.

This recollection of a solitary image with little, if any, associated scientific understanding of what the phenomenon was intended to show has also been reported by Berry et al. (1999) who found that while practical work can provide pupils with images of a particular phenomenon these images had limited value and were not necessarily indicative of high-level mental engagement with the practical task.

Similarly pupil recollections about procedures tend to relate to *what* they did rather than *why* they did it as the following example illustrates:

Researcher: Do you remember any practical that you did longer ago?

SH5: Yeah we got like different chemicals in the tubes like blue liquids and then put like a red in with them and see what they turned out like.

SH6: Yeah you mix a and b, like copper sulphate and something else, and you mix it like together.

Researcher: And that was to help you learn what?

SH6: I don't know really. [Both pupils are laughing loudly.]

SH5: [Shrugs shoulders and shakes head to indicate that they do not know.]

Researcher: What practicals do you remember doing?

SH7: Distilling stuff.

SH8: Yeah.

Researcher: What did you distil, crude oil?

SH7: Yeah a blue liquid.

SH8: Yeah it was a blue liquid.

SH7: Just a blue liquid, we don't know what it was, just a blue liquid and we got . water out of it.

Researcher: You got water out of it, how did that work?

SH7: Well we got a bottle.

SH8: We put a liquid in it, put a thermometer in it, put it on a tripod, put a Bunsen burner under it and it went through all the tubes in place and it went into a test tube in a beaker.

SH7: Hot water went into a beaker.

SH8: Yeah.

SH7: And if the temperature goes over too far, over a hundred, you had to take it out and then hold on a bit and then have another go.

In this respect their recollections, and in the latter example just mentioned these are relatively detailed procedural recollections, appear to reflect the emphasis – in terms of teaching time – placed by many of the teachers on getting the pupils to successfully *do* what they intended with objects and materials, in order to produce a particular phenomenon, rather than on ensuring that they necessarily understood *why* they were doing it in the manner specified by the teacher and/or worksheet. What this example also illustrates is that while one of the pupils (SH7) was able to recollect a precise temperature range – a range that the teacher might have been expected to emphasize in order to ensure that the pupils produced the desired phenomena – there was no evidence that they understood *why* this temperature range was required.

A similar lack of understanding was observed in the task used by Mr Oldstead in which he intended the pupils to produce a change of state cooling curve for a waxy material (octadecanol) by recording its temperature on a regular basis as it cooled and then plotting the data on a graph. Here, although the pupils followed a completely closed 'recipe' style task, the procedure, as it appeared on the blackboard, differed from that provided verbally during the teacher demonstration. The written instructions specified that the wax was to be heated to 75°C (a temperature just above its melting point) and for the temperature to then be recorded every minute until it had cooled to 35°C. In contrast, the verbal instructions stipulated that the wax was to be heated until it melted and went clear and for the pupils to seek the teacher's advice on when to stop recording the temperature. While a quarter of that lesson was devoted to ensuring that the pupils knew what they were to do with the objects and materials, no time was devoted to getting them to think about the initial heating simply as a means to liquefy the wax, or to understand that the value of 75°C was simply a guide temperature that corresponded to liquefied wax slightly above its melting point. The fact that the written and verbal instructions were essentially the same, albeit expressed in a slightly different manner, was not understood by all of the pupils, many of whom saw the value of 75°C as critical and devoted considerable time to ensuring that the wax was at, or as near as possible to, this temperature before starting to record their data. In the following extract it can be seen that while one of the pupils (OD3) attached greater importance to the written instructions another pupil (OD2) argued that there was no need to get the wax to exactly 75°C. However, it is important to note, and can be seen from their comments, that their primary – if not sole – reason for doing so was that they attributed greater significance to the teacher's verbal, as opposed to written, instructions and there was no evidence that they understood *why* the starting temperature was not critical:

> OD1: Tell me when to start the timing.
>
> OD2: I will.
>
> OD3: Has it actually melted yet?
>
> OD2: It's melting look it's getting a lot smaller, when it gets to 70.
>
> OD3: [Addressing OD2] No, no, not 70 [points to the blackboard] 75, it says on the board.
>
> OD2: One, it doesn't need to be exact just as close as we can get it to 75 or when, no he [Mr Oldstead] said when it gets to a clear liquid not 75.
>
> OD3: Ok, alright then [raising voice] turn it off then. [Shakes their head to indicate that they still disagree with this course of action.]

As a consequence of this lack of understanding, and the fact that many of the pupils devoted considerably more time to getting the wax to within a degree or two of the suggested temperature than was really necessary, Mr Oldstead had to abandon his aim of getting the pupils to plot their data in order for them to observe (and subsequently explain) the characteristic plateau shape of a change of state cooling curve.

While the above example illustrates how a failure to adequately explain *why* something is being done, in contrast to *what* is to be done, can prevent pupils from learning what the teacher intended, so too can a failure to produce the desired phenomena and/or data. What I would argue is that while the successful production of a phenomenon is a necessary condition for learning to occur it is not, by itself, sufficient to ensure that the pupils learn what the teacher intends them to learn about observables. Certainly those tasks in which the teacher intends the pupils to learn about relationships between observables are particularly dependent upon the need to ensure that they successfully produce the desired phenomena. In those tasks in which the phenomena were not, for one reason or another, produced – and these have been discussed in Chapter 3 – the tasks were ineffective in getting the pupils to learn about a particular relationship between the observables. In a task where the pupils appeared to have no idea as to what to expect, as was the case with pupils in Mrs Risplith's class who gave no indication of knowing that pulse rate and heart rate should have the same value, the fact that many of the pupils did *not* find these values to be clearly and unambiguously the same meant that they were resistant to the teacher's claims that they were:

Researcher: Do you think your heart and pulse rate will be the same?
RH6: I think not.
Researcher: What has this practical helped you understand?
RH6: That we're alive and that we've got a pulse.
Researcher: What has this practical helped you understand?
RH2: It's helping me to see that the heart beat is beating more than the pulse (*sic*).

Researcher: Were you expecting the heart rate and the pulse to be the same?
RH5: I didn't know really.

Yet there were tasks in which the pupils clearly did have initial ideas about what they thought they would observe and these expectations were not supported by the data that they produced. Consider, for example, the task on electromagnets in which Dr Kepwick's intention was for the pupils to learn about the relationship between the number of turns on an electromagnet coil and the number of paperclips that it would be able to support. Here the expectation of many of the pupils prior to their undertaking the task was, if only on the basis of the generic idea that 'more of x means bigger and/or stronger y' (Stavy and Tirosh, 1996), that the number of paperclips that could be suspended by the electromagnet would increase as the number of turns on the coil was increased.

What was found, and similar findings have been reported in previous studies (Driver et al., 1985; Gunstone and Watts, 2000; Shipstone, 2000; Solomon, 1988), was that the idea, in this case that 'more of x means bigger and/or stronger y', was sufficiently resilient that the pupils' observation of a 'discrepant event' (Nussbaum, 2000 p. 143), while confusing, did not generate any cognitive conflict (Driver et al., 1985). Instead what was found was that the pupils explained the 'discrepant results' away by suggesting that the equipment was not working properly, in a manner reminiscent of the way in which Millar (2004) suggests that some teachers 'engage in the rhetoric of "explaining away" the observations, perhaps appealing to notions of "experimental error" or poor equipment' (p. 5):

Researcher: How's yours going?

KK9: We've just got one.

Researcher: What's your question? [KK10 had raised their hand]

KK10: Why's it [points to equipment] not working?

Researcher: It's not working?

KK9: Well it's working, but not as you would expect it to.

Researcher: How would you expect it to?

KK9: Well with more coils you'd have more magnetism yeah because there's more energy going around the thing so it's more magnetic.

Researcher: But you haven't found that?

KK9: No.

Researcher: Now does that confuse you when it doesn't work?

KK9: Yeah.

KK10: Yes because it's the same for all of them. [Each coil had only attracted 1 paper clip.]

KK13: It's broken [indicates equipment].

Researcher: It couldn't have been broken because it has worked hasn't it?

KK14: We think it might not have worked as well as it could do.

KK13: Yeah there's something wrong with it. [Points to electromagnet.]

KK14: That one [pointing to result for 20 turn coil] should have been more than that one [pointing to identical result for 2 turn coil] because there's more energy but it didn't.

Although Driver et al. (1985) have suggested that the observation of a discrepant event 'is not necessarily followed by a restructuring of that student's ideas – such restructuring takes time and favourable circumstances' (p. 6), this clearly does not preclude the possibility that some pupils will restructure their ideas – unfortunately not always to ones that are scientifically correct – on the basis of a single (sometimes discrepant) event. The following transcript illustrates how two pupils, who had initially believed that an electromagnet with more coils would support more paperclips, restructured their ideas claiming to have learnt, as a direct consequence of failing to produce the results intended by the teacher, that fewer coils would (erroneously from a scientific point of view) support more paperclips:

Researcher: How's yours going?

KK7: Not very well.

Researcher: What have you found?

KK7: We haven't.

Researcher: So [looking at their table of results] with 10 coils you held 3 paper clips and with 20 you held 1 now is that what you predicted?

KK8: Well we thought that with more coils it would be more magnetism but it's obviously not.

Researcher: Why did you think that?

KK8: Because I thought if there were more wire there'd be more electricity.

Researcher: But you don't think that's right now?

KK7: No.

Researcher: So by using this practical you now know that more coils is less powerful [points to table of results] whereas you had thought that it would have been more?

KK7: Yes.

KK8: Yeah.

Researcher: [Watching them test an electromagnet with 2 coils.] Now you've managed to get 1 [paperclip] with 2 coils.

KK8: Now I can't understand that.

Researcher: What don't you understand?

KK7: Well that with only 2 coils it's 1 [paperclip] and with 20 it's 1 and with 10 it's 3.

Researcher: Why's that confusing you?

KK7: Because I would have thought it would have been more for 2.

Researcher: Why?

KK7: Because if it's going [they have identified a trend albeit an incorrect one] up I'd have thought it would have been more for that [points to 2 coil result] instead of that [points to 10 coil result].

The problem with this task, as with a small number of others, was that relatively few pupils managed to produce the desired phenomena and/or data. In these situations it is very difficult for the teacher 'to appeal to the norm within the class: what did *most* students find?' (Millar, 2004 p. 5) as a means of 'averaging away' the few 'problematic' results. Yet in one such task the teacher, Mrs Risplith, while keen to avoid the introduction of 'exemplary data' (Gott and Duggan, 1996 p. 801) to replace that generated by the pupils, also wanted to avoid the confusion that would arise regarding the relationship between two observables – pulse rate and heart rate – were the pupils to use their own results. To overcome this problem Mrs Risplith, having placed all of the results on the board, began to 'explain away' those results that were most notably at odds with the relationship that she intended them to 'discover' for themselves:

> Mrs Risplith: What do you notice about these two? [Points to 106 and 90 and then 97 and 108.] We're not happy with these results, they seem way out. What do you notice about the figures compared to the others?
> RHa: They're really high.
> Mrs Risplith: Really high. Well done. So when your heartbeat is high . . .
> RHb: [Interrupting] You're dying.
> Mrs Risplith: Do you think it's easier or more difficult to measure it?
> RH19: More difficult.
> Mrs Risplith: It'll be more difficult, which might explain the difference in these readings. [Draws a line through these two pair of 'problematic' results to indicate that they can be disregarded as well as another pair of dissimilar results although no reason for doing this is given.].

In contrast Dr Kepwick, who was aware that the overwhelming majority of pupils had failed to produce the desired data, judiciously selected the results of one pair of pupils which she knew exemplified the desired relationship:

> Dr Kepwick: Unfortunately some people [in fact almost all] had problems with the fuses on their power packs, but other people managed to get quite dramatic results. So [addressing KK19 by name] can you tell me what you got?
> KK19: 2 [paperclips] for 2 [turns], 12 for 10 and 23 for 20.

Table 4.5 Dr Kepwick's completed results table

Number of coils		2	10	20
Number of paperclips picked up		2	12	23
	Metal core		No metal core	
Number of paperclips picked up	Better		Worse	

These results, that showed the relationship between the observables that Dr Kepwick was keen for the pupils to discover, were then entered on to the results table on the board (Table 4.5) that the pupils were then required to copy down.

While Dr Kepwick subsequently asked other pupils to state their results, she made no comment about the fact that most of these showed no discernible correlation between the number of turns on the core and the number of paperclips picked up. Rather than stating, in the face of what was clearly the overwhelming evidence to the contrary, that the number of paperclips that could be suspended from the end of the electromagnet increased with the number of turns on the coil, Dr Kepwick asked the same pupil, whose results she had used for the data in the table, to summarize what they had learnt from the task:

> Dr Kepwick: So [addressing KK19 by name], what are we going to take away from this lesson remembering about electromagnets?
> KK19: The more coils you have the more electricity, the higher the number of paper clips.

Dr Kepwick appeared reluctant to either accept or reject this summary because, as she made clear in the interview after the lesson, she did not fully understand the underlying physics:

> Dr Kepwick: Like when the lad [KK19] said about more current flowing through the wires. Well the current doesn't actually change, does it? In that the current coming out of the power pack is still the same and all these things I'm like asking myself, and thinking 'just don't focus on that' because I'm not entirely sure.

The above examples illustrate how, in a small number of tasks, the pupils were unable to *learn* what the teacher intended about observables simply because the task was ineffective in terms of getting the pupils to produce the desired phenomena. However, as most of the tasks observed were effective in getting the pupils to do what the teacher intended with observables and, as such, enabled the overwhelming majority of them not only to produce the desired phenomena and/or data but to learn what the teacher intended them to learn about observables.

Yet what can be seen (Tables 4.2, 4.3 and 4.4) is that even if it is assumed that most of the tasks undertaken by the pupils prior to this study were as effective in enabling the pupils to successfully produce the intended phenomena as most of those observed – arguably a reasonable assumption given the wide-spread and frequent use of closed tasks – this success will not be reflected in the pupils' medium or long-term ability to recollect what the teacher had intended them to learn about observables.

That pupils' recollections provide an insight into what they retain from a learning activity – something that can subsequently be used to evaluate the effectiveness of the practical task – can be seen in the following examples. In both of these tasks – involving the chromatographic separation of dyes – the teachers (Miss Nunwick and Mr Saltmarsh) simply intended the pupils to produce and witness a phenomenon. In both cases what the teacher intended was, as Mr Saltmarsh informed me, 'for the pupils to see that food dyes, that appeared to be only one colour, were in fact made up of a mixture of different colours'. Given that both tasks were effective in enabling the pupils to successfully produce the phenomenon of chromatographic separation all of the pupils were able to 'see' what their teacher intended. Indeed, when these pupils were questioned to ascertain what they had learnt (in the case of Miss Nunwick, the learning related not only to this particular task but also to two, and in some cases three, previous occasions on which they had undertaken the chromatographic separation of dyes), all of their responses clearly suggested that these relatively simple learning objectives had been achieved:

NK8: I expect it to go up with the water until it's almost at the top. It should change colour, each pen should give a different type of streaks of colour.
Researcher: Why did it change colour?
NK9: Is it 'cause there's different colours made of black, there's different colours going into black, making black, and they're just separating.

Researcher: What have you learnt?

NK15: There's different inks in different pens [of the same colour].

Mr Saltmarsh: What do your results mean? But already you can say something can't you about these lines and colours. What can you say about those colours even now before we've finished the experiment?

SHb: Two colours are coming out from the ink.

However, not only did the pupils appear to learn what the teacher intended about observables but it appeared, from the comments of some of the pupils, that some of this knowledge was being recollected from previous tasks on chromatographic separation – tasks that had been presented in the novel context of a murder mystery:

Researcher: Have you done this before?

NK11: Yeah, we did it on induction day.

Researcher: So you've done this before, do you remember it?

NK11: Yeah, quite well.

Researcher: What do you remember about it?

NK11: They made it up to be like a crime investigation thing.

NK12: A murder thing.

Researcher: What do you think this practical [they had yet to produce a chromatogram] is meant to show you?

NK11: That you think something's pure but it's not actually pure.

NK12: All the different elements in it have different colours I think.

NK11: Yeah, that are making it up are separating as the water's going up it's gathering them apart.

Researcher: What do you think this is going to show?

NK3: That different, different, pens have different mixtures of colours in them

Researcher: Right. Why do you expect that? I mean how do you know that?

NK3: Did it before.

Researcher: You've done it before?

NK3: Yeah.

Researcher: Oh, when have you done this before?

NK3: We did it on our induction day as a murder thing [end of Summer term Year 6] and last year [Year 7] and in Year 3. [The pupil claimed that their teacher had demonstrated this at primary school.]

Researcher: Really? So you've done this three times before this, and so you already know what you're going to get. Is this [addressing NK4] the same with you?

NK4: Yeah.

Again, what the these examples illustrate is how the novel context of a murder investigation provides an effective anchor for the recollection, not of ideas as White (1979) has suggested, but of the observable features of the phenomenon itself. This finding was supported by the fact that other pupils, undertaking what were arguably 'ordinary' tasks – 'ordinary' is used here as the antonym of 'unusual' – while able to recollect having previously undertaken the same practical were unable to recollect the phenomena and/or data that they had produced:

Researcher: Now have you done this experiment before? [Mr Normanby had informed the researcher that they had.]

NY5: No I don't think so.

NY6: Yeah we have a couple of years ago.

Researcher: Do you remember what happened?

NY5: No not really, no.

Researcher: Have you done this experiment, or a similar one to this, in physics a few weeks ago?

UF16: Yeah.

UF17: Yes, yeah we did actually but it was with erm, I've forgotten which metal and what we found.

Researcher: But you did it?

UF17: Yeah I remember we did it.

While the successful production of a particular phenomenon and/or data is a necessary requirement if the pupils are to *learn* what the teacher intends about observables, the ability to *recollect* what has been learnt appears, as can be seen in Tables 4.2, 4.3 and 4.4, to be correlated with whether or not the task was, in some sense, unusual. Indeed, as previously discussed, some of the most frequent and vividly recollected tasks were those relating to the visually spectacular teacher demonstrations of the reactivity of group one metals and the Thermite reaction in which the phenomena, successfully produced by the teacher, were observed by all of the pupils. Yet it is important to recognize, given that the pupils were just as able to recollect the visually spectacular burning of magnesium ribbon, or the making of a model suspension bridge, which they carried out for themselves, that it was the 'unusualness' of the task, rather than whether it was demonstrated by the teacher or undertaken by the pupils, that appears to be the critical factor in determining whether or not it is recollected. In this respect the relevance of 'unusualness', rather than the teaching tactic itself, may help to explain why previous studies (Thijs and Bosch, 1995; Garrett and Roberts, 1982; Kruglak and Wall, 1959) found no significant difference in retention rates between pupils undertaking small-group practical work and those observing the same tasks as teacher demonstrations.

You might think, as I have suggested, that pupils are better able to recollect those tasks that are in some sense 'unusual', that a promising approach would therefore be to ensure that *all* of your practical work is unusual. Yet were you to do so my expectation (and this is not something I have tried – although please feel free to try this and let me know what you find) would be that the unusual would simply cease to be unusual any more and only those tasks deemed as being 'extremely' unusual would then be remembered.

Learning about ideas

Learning in the domain of ideas, as Millar (2004) suggests, 'is not discovery or construction of something new and unknown; rather it is making what others already know your own'. (p. 6). In this respect the role of practical work in the teaching and learning of science content is, as we have seen in Chapter 3, to help pupils develop a link (Figure 3.3) between the domain of observables and the domain of ideas (Millar et al., 1999; Brodin, 1978).

Yet in order to succeed in linking these two domains of knowledge it is necessary for pupils to have access to both and, in order for this to occur, they must be helped, not only to produce the phenomenon, but, equally importantly, to think about their observations in a particular way (Lunetta, 1998; Gunstone, 1991). Yet what was found, Tobin (1990) has also reported similar findings, was that because 'most teachers seem to be preoccupied with management in laboratory activities' (p. 414) frequently little, if any, time is devoted to helping pupils to think about the phenomena using the ideas that the teachers intended them to use. And yet, as Gunstone (1991) makes clear, 'for practical work to have any serious effect on student theory reconstruction and linking of concepts in different ways, the students need to spend more time interacting with ideas and less time interacting with apparatus' (p. 74). Certainly because many pupils lack, or do not know how to apply, the relevant scientific ideas that their teachers intend them to use, they are unable to form the link between the phenomena and associated scientific ideas that would enable them to understand the former in terms of the latter. As Hodson (1992) has pointed out 'It is clear that a child who lacks the appropriate theoretical understandings will not know where to look, or how to look, in order to make observations appropriate to the task in hand, or how to interpret what she/he sees' (p. 68).

The lack of an effective link between these two domains of knowledge may help to explain why the recollection of an observation in the domain of observables (Tables 4.2, 4.3 and 4.4) did not provide, as White (1991) has claimed that it could, 'a strong peg which maintains . . . the easy recallability of the associated verbal knowledge' (p. 385). Hart et al. (2000) have also reported finding little evidence among Year 10 pupils of any attempt to link and explain their observations using scientific knowledge that they already possessed. While the findings of Hart et al. (2000) relate specifically to practical tasks in which the pupils have been taught about the scientific ideas needed to help them understand their observations *before* undertaking the practical task, they too suggest that even when pupils have (or are assumed to have) access to the two domains of knowledge they still find it extremely difficult to form links between them.

What did pupils learn about ideas?

Even when the pupils were guided towards forming links between the two domains, as was the case with Dr Starbeck who devoted more time in the lesson to 'doing with ideas' than to 'doing with observables', there was no evidence that any of the Year 11 pupils, all of whom had undertaken the same task the previous year, were able to recollect either the observables, or ideas, or the links between them that Dr Starbeck had intended. However, many of these same Year 11 pupils were able to recollect an 'unusual' practical activity, also on the topic of current conservation and voltage, which they had undertaken at about the same time the previous year. It should be noted that while this task was referred to by the pupils in their recollections as a 'practical', it was a non-practical activity because at no point were the pupils required to observe, or manipulate, real objects. This task was unusual in so far as it required the pupils to form 'circuits' by rearranging the laboratory tabletops on which they were then required to walk or stand, using a form of drama referred to as 'acting out' (Braund, 1999), in order to 'act out' the role of electrons, ammeters, voltmeters, a battery and lamps, with a pile of cardboard boxes being used to represent the energy supplied by the battery to the electrons. This activity, one of the most frequently recollected, supports the view of the National Curriculum Council (1989) that 'When pupils act out incidents the experience can help them to remember' (Section C16, 9.3). However, their recollections related only to the unusual nature of the activity – especially being allowed to walk on the tables – and/or to what they themselves had been required to do in terms of acting out, and provided no link to the scientific ideas that both this task, and the one that immediately preceded it, were designed to help develop as the following examples illustrate.

SW4: One to do with electric circuits. We put all the tables together so that they made, so that they made, they were the wires.

SW5: Yeah we had to walk on the tables with boxes and people had to pretend to be voltmeters.

Researcher: What did it show you?

SW5: [Laughter] I don't know.

SW4: [Shakes head to indicate that they too do not know].

SW7: One practical I do remember was an investigation of electrons and he [Dr Starbeck] put all the tables in a big square and he made us lot be like electrons. And that's, that's made me, made me remember it because of how different it was to just er practical.

SW9: Last year we did this unusual one where we put the tables together and we had to be electrons and walk around on the tables.

SW8: When we were doing circuits we joined all the tables together and used those boxes there [points to a pile of boxes under a side bench] and we had to be electrons on tables and when you walked past the person who was supposed to be the battery they gave you the box and you walked around and you came to the lamp and you gave it to the lamp and you walk back round and got another box from the battery, and you walked round and you gave it to the lamp and when all the boxes are gone the battery's dead.

It should be noted that, other than in the case of one pupil (SW5) where it was possible that their recollection of this activity was triggered by the recollection of their partner (SW4), all of the other pupils recollected this activity without having heard the recollection of any other pupil during interviews during a practical lesson that had no connection to that topic. However, even though many of the Year 11 pupils, who had undertaken the task in Year 10, were able to recollect what they *did*, generally without any 'triggering', none were able to recollect the scientific ideas that Dr Starbeck had informed the researcher he intended the task to develop: namely that electric charge is conserved and that these charges transfer energy from the battery to the bulb where it is transformed into light and heat energy. While one pupil (SW8) was able to describe the non-scientific model of the electric circuit, there was no evidence of their being able to link this with the appropriate, though relatively difficult (Shipstone, 2000; Driver, et al., 1994), scientific ideas that the task had been designed to develop. Even those pupils who were able to recollect the term 'electron' only used it to describe their role within the drama rather than to represent, as the teacher intended, the idea of a negatively charged particle, the movement of which constitutes an electric current.

Indeed many of those pupils who made the general claim that practical tasks helped them to recollect information did so because they appeared to equate 'learning' with the ability to provide a very brief qualitative description of what they had done and/or seen with observables in a few tasks that contained a memorable episode:

> DE10: I learn more if I do rather than watching someone else.
> Researcher: Can you remember any other practicals that you've done?
> [Pupils shake their heads to indicate no.] Even in Year 7?
> DE9: Oh yes we did this, made this, cell bag thing.
> DE10: Oh yeah [nodding head to indicate that they too now remember] with wallpaper paste.
> DE9: I learnt loads from that.
> Researcher: Wallpaper paste?
> DE9: Oh yeah. [Grimaces and indicates manipulating something sticky with their fingers.]
> DE10: Yeah, you had to make these cell bags.
> DE9: Yeah and I learnt loads from that.
> Researcher: What did you learn?
> DE9: Everything.
> Researcher: What?
> DE9: 'cause I got top marks.
> Researcher: Ok, but what did you learn, can you tell me?
> DE9: Well I've forgotten.

Pupils undertaking food tests, who had initially claimed to learn more from practical tasks than from alternative teaching strategies, still thought it unlikely that they would recollect details of the test for starch after a period of as little as six months:

> Researcher: Do you like doing practical work?
> UE6: Yeah because I think you learn more than writing out of a textbook.
> Researcher: Do you think if I was to come back in six months time and ask you how do you test for starch, what do you use? [Pupils laugh.]
> UE7: We'd probably have forgotten.
> UE6: Yeah.

Although the teachers' intended learning objectives for most of the tasks recollected by the pupils (Tables 4.2, 4.3 and 4.4) must remain a matter of conjecture many of these would, it seems reasonable to assume, have included learning objectives within the domain of ideas. However, while the teachers might have intended the pupils to learn about certain ideas, and indeed in some cases they might actually have been successful in getting the pupils to do so, there was no evidence that they were able to subsequently recollect these ideas and so the pupils were unaware of having learnt them. These findings support previous claims (Gott and Duggan, 1996; Watson et al., 1995; Clackson and Wright, 1992; White, 1991; Gunstone and Champagne, 1990; Brophy, 1983; Moreira, 1980) all of which have reported that pupils appear to learn relatively little about the ideas that the practical tasks were designed to illustrate.

Review

While these findings are, I would suggest, by no means a resounding endorsement of the use of practical work as a means of teaching and learning science content (scientific ideas), it must be recognized that such teaching and learning is likely to be difficult to achieve no matter what tactic is used. Indeed, as Hofstein and Lunetta (1982) have emphasized, many studies that have compared practical work

> with more conventional classroom teaching over relatively short periods of time . . . have reported nonsignificant results, meaning that the laboratory medium was at least as effective in promoting student growth on the variable measured as were more conventional modes of instruction. (p. 212)

It might therefore be argued that although practical work may be no more (or less) effective at getting the pupils to learn about science content than other teaching tactics, the very fact that pupils frequently claim to find it less boring, and more enjoyable, than such non-practical alternatives is, in itself, a positive factor in its favour. However, given the disproportionately high cost of providing practical work in secondary schools (Clackson and Wright, 1992) and the claim by White (1996) that 'whether laboratories enthuse students or not, few governments, private societies or individuals run schools to provide enjoyment' (p. 761) means that claims regarding both its effectiveness and its affective value need to be uppermost in your mind when thinking about its use in one of your lessons.

In the next chapter I want to consider the strategies for getting pupils to think about the objects, materials and ideas in the way that their teacher intended. To do this I will focus on a specific lesson that exemplifies some of the suggestions I have made for making a practical task effective at both levels 1 and 2 and across both domains.

Strategies for Getting Pupils to Think about the Objects, Materials and Ideas

5

Introduction

In this chapter I want to draw on a very effective physics practical lesson as a means of illustrating what I consider to be good practice in terms of getting pupils to think about the objects, materials and ideas. As I draw quite extensively on this example I think it worth providing some background detail regarding the teacher, the class, the lesson and, in particular, the practical task embedded within that lesson.

The teacher

Dr Starbeck, the teacher selected, is atypical – both in comparison to the other teachers involved in this study and to teachers nationally. He has been teaching for more than twenty years and has held the posts of head of physics and head of science. He has a research degree in the subject that he was teaching in this lesson (physics), has achieved Advanced Skills Teacher status, and has also been awarded a national prize in recognition of his teaching. Furthermore he has been involved in various science education initiatives, originating at university level, and is familiar with a wide range of educational research literature that has, he claims, not only informed his practice but caused him to challenge some of the widely accepted beliefs about the teaching of science and, in particular, the use and role of practical work.

Pupils – class and small groups

The Year 10, set 2 of 5 [middle to low academic ability group], had 26 pupils comprising 14 boys and 12 girls. Dr Starbeck informed me that all of the pupils within this class would be entered for the foundation tier, double award, GCSE paper in which most would be expected to achieve grade 'C'. None of the pupils within the class were registered as having special educational needs or behavioural problems. The pupils sat with and formed their own small groups on the basis of peer friendships with, they informed me, the composition of these groups changing only infrequently during the course of the academic year.

The practical task as intended by the teacher

Dr Starbeck's aims for the practical task were that it would reinforce a model of electric current that he would introduce at the start of the lesson and, in so doing, help the pupils to understand that:

(i) An electric current is the flow of charges around a circuit.
(ii) Ammeters measure current that is, they are 'charge counters'.
(iii) Charges carry energy around the circuit.
(iv) Current is not used up.
(v) The energy carried by the charges is lost to the circuit when it is transformed into other forms of energy e.g. heat and light in a bulb.
(vi) Voltmeters measure the difference in the energy carried by a charge between two different points in a circuit.

The task would require the pupils to construct a simple series circuit containing two bulbs from a circuit diagram that would be projected onto a screen. Having constructed the circuit, and adjusted the power supply to the voltage stipulated, they would, using an ammeter, take three reading of the current: one on either side of the two bulbs and one between them.

The pupils would draw a circuit diagram to accompany each reading and the value of the current was to be noted next to the circuit diagram. If this was completed, the pupils were then to investigate the effect of decreasing the voltage on the size of the current as well as any effect this might have upon the appearance of the bulbs.

While it was not possible to assess what these pupils were able to recollect either in the medium or long term, as the lowest level indicator of what they might have learnt, this lesson did provide a clear example as to how practical work can be designed to help pupils to 'do' with, and learn about, ideas, as well as about objects, materials and phenomena. So while this lesson 'proves' that this is possible – and does actually occur – the evidence from this study is that it is all too rare.

Strategies in action

One strategy used effectively by Dr Starbeck to ensure that his pupils could still manage to produce the desired phenomena, despite his devoting a relatively large proportion of the lesson time to familiarizing them with the ideas that he intended them to use, was for the practical task to be short, relatively simple, and require little in terms of procedural information. The task itself was not designed to occupy a whole lesson – as is frequently the case – but was instead a constituent part of, and embedded with, a whole science lesson. The practical was, in this respect, not seen as an end in itself but rather as an integral part of the total means of achieving that end:

> Dr Starbeck: The point of it really is not that it's a complicated piece of practical work but it gives them a vehicle to use that thinking model.

Furthermore the task presentation, although relatively short in duration, was directed specifically at those areas that experience had shown were liable to perceived as problematic by the pupils. The procedural instructions therefore focused on the use of power packs, ammeters and voltmeters – including how to connect them into the circuit and the need to ignore any minus signs that appeared when taking ammeter and/or voltmeter readings:

Researcher: You stressed [to the pupils] that the minus sign wasn't important.

Dr Starbeck: Well that's me trying to clear away the clutter so they can focus on what I want them to focus on which is the model. And I know the minus sign is clutter and I know they'll spend ages worrying about it.

Researcher: How do you know that?

Dr Starbeck: Because in the past, when I've done it badly, they've worried about the minus signs. Minus signs are clutter.

Pre-empting procedural problems meant that the significant amount of time that would have needed to be spent moving around the laboratory sorting out these problems with small groups of pupils was instead spent on the development of a non-scientific model that provided the pupils with the opportunity to think about and discuss the task using ideas and language with which they were already familiar. In this case the non-scientific model involved an animated cartoon character (Figure 5.1) who walked around a rectangular path and, as s/he did so, had to pass through a giant light bulb.

At the top of the path, under the circuit symbol for a cell, was a pile of boxes. Each time the person walked under the symbol for the cell they picked up a box and carried this with them as they walked around the path. As the person walked through the giant bulb the box that they carried vanished and the bulb emitted a flash of light. The person then continued around the path back to the symbol of the cell where, having picked up another box, the cycle is repeated.

Figure 5.1 A diagram of the animated circuit model

In the first part of the lesson Dr Starbeck devoted 'whole class' time to discussing the familiar objects in the non-scientific model and subsequently used these objects as a means of scaffolding (Wood, et al., 1976) the corresponding entities within the scientific model of a simple series circuit:

Dr Starbeck: [Points to the animated character moving around a stylized circuit on the whiteboard.] Right so we've got something moving around a circuit, a person moves around the circuit. What's moving around a real electric circuit?

SK4: Electrons.

Dr Starbeck: Ok, electrons, electric charges. So the person, [points to character on screen], stands for?

SK5 Charge . . .

Dr Starbeck: What do people stand for?

SK13: Charges.

Dr Starbeck: [Addressing SK14] What do the people stand for?

SK14: Electrons, charges.

Dr Starbeck: Electrons, charges. People stand for charges. [Points to animated character walking around circuit.] What do charges do? They move around the circuit. What do we call a movement of charge? [This had been taught in the previous lesson.]

SK14: Current.

Dr Starbeck: Current. Current right. So we've got charges moving around a circuit, people carrying boxes, charges carrying energy round the circuit. Ok?

By using the non-scientific model as a scaffold Dr Starbeck got the pupils to think and talk about an ammeter, initially as a device that counts people – he drew the 'A' symbol for an ammeter on the blackboard like a person with arms and legs – and then, drawing on the analogy in which people correspond to charges within the scientific model, encouraged the pupils to think about the function of the ammeter as being to count charges.

The important issue here is not that of whether, when asked, the pupils made correct predictions about what they thought they would observe when they undertook the task, but whether they thought about the task using the ideas intended by the teacher. In fact, initially, many of the pupils' predications reflected an attenuation model in which current is consumed (Shipstone, 2000). Yet what I found, moving around the laboratory, was that as the pupils' familiarity and confidence with the use of the scientific terminology/ideas increased during the course of the lesson many of them began to replace colloquial terms, used in the non-scientific model, with the appropriate scientific terms used within the scientific model, as the two following examples illustrate:

Researcher: What's your prediction?

SK7: Well I thought it would be all the same.

Researcher: Why is that?

SK7: It's the people [pauses], like the charge just keeps going round and then collects energy at the battery.

Researcher: So you don't expect any change?

SK7: No, not really . . .

Researcher: What have you found?

SK5: I was wrong. [Their initial prediction was based on a current attenuation model.] They all stayed the same except for one where it went up a tiny little bit.

Researcher: So what's that told you?

SK5: That amps don't really change.

Researcher: And what are the amps measuring in the model you're using?

SK5: The amount of charge going round. The number of people's not changing . . .

Although the majority of pupils continued to use a mixture of scientific and colloquial terminology there were a small number of pupils whom, by the end of the task, were able to discuss all aspects of the task using the appropriate scientific terminology, a feature associated with language usage at level v:

Researcher: So what's the voltmeter actually measuring?

SK21: The energy.

Researcher: [Directing the question to SK22.] So this voltmeter that you've connected across a bulb, what's it measuring?

SK22: How much energy is going in, and how much energy is coming out.

Researcher: And what will that tell you?

SK22: How much energy it has lost . . .

While not unique in intending his pupils to think about the task using specific ideas Dr Starbeck was the only teacher, among all those observed, who devoted so much of the lesson time to ensuring that the pupils were not only introduced to the appropriate scientific terminology but that they understood what they meant and were able to use it appropriately (language levels iv and v). I want, at this point, to compare Dr Starbeck's lesson with a lesson taught by Miss Kilburn, within the framework of the Cognitive Acceleration through Science Education (CASE) programme (Adey et al., 1989), which is a clear example of a practical lesson specifically designed to help pupils make links between some abstract ideas and some concrete examples. Unlike Dr Starbeck, Miss Kilburn spoke of the pressure to ensure that all of her pupils would be able to produce the desired phenomena and so chose to devote a lot of whole class lesson time to procedural instructions. As a consequence Miss Kilburn was able to spend only a relatively brief period of time explaining to the pupils what the central terms 'input variable' and 'output variable' meant. As a consequence, as their comments that follow show, many of them simply failed to understand the meaning of the two central terms that would have been needed for the practical work to effectively bridge the two domains of knowledge:

> Miss Kilburn: Now what we're going to do today is take variables a bit further and we're going to decide whether a variable is an input variable or an output variable. Now an input variable is always going to be one that you change. Ok that is going to be your input variable. Now your output variable is going to be the one that changes as a result of what you've changed. So if we go back to our indigestion powder [a practical task undertaken two week earlier] which one did you change in this experiment? [No response from the pupils.] Which one did we decide was a factor and change? [Still no response from any of the pupils.] In order to work out the best way to cure indigestion?

Despite many of the pupils' evident lack of familiarity with, and understanding of, the terms 'input' and 'output' variable, in a task that was primarily designed to get the pupils thinking about and using these terms, Miss Kilburn made no further attempt to clarify them instead devoting a lot of time to sorting out procedural issues an a small group by group basis. Indeed I found that it was their lack of familiarity and understanding of these terms that meant that many of the pupils were simply unable, and/or unwilling, to think about the task using the ideas of input and output variables:

> Researcher: So what's the output variable?
> KN4: What does that mean?
> Researcher: So for you this lesson is all about how many weights it takes to pull this [the pulley] down to the bottom and it doesn't have much to do with input and output variables.
> KN15: It'd help if we knew what they were . . .
>
> Researcher: Ok, can you tell me what's the input variable in this task?
> KN13: No.
> KN12: [Shakes head in the negative.]
> Researcher: You don't know, that's ok. What's the output variable? [Both pupils shrug and shake their heads in the negative.] Could you explain what they [an input and output variable] are to me?
> KN13: I don't know.
> Researcher: [To KN12.] Do you know?
> KN12: No . . .
>
> Researcher: What are you thinking of when you're doing this task?
> KN11: Nothing really.
> KN10: It's boring . . .

Given that many of the pupils were unclear about what the terms 'input' and 'output' variable meant their discussions tended to focus on observables and procedural issues (level iii) with none of the pupils being heard to use the term 'input' and 'output' variable when talking about their observations unless prompted to do so by the researcher:

> Researcher: [Addressing pupils who had, after almost 4 minutes of the five allocated, still not managed to obtain any readings.] Right, what have we got here?
> KN6: [Points to pulleys] We're doing pulleys.
> KN7: [Points to scale on Newton-metre.] We haven't really started yet, were just trying to get some weights on 'cause at the moment it isn't at zero and we don't know how to change it back? [Pupils appear unaware that the hook that holds the weight has a mass of 50 grams and it is this that is causing the non-zero reading.]
> Researcher: Must it be at zero?
> KN6: Yes because then it'll give you an accurate reading.
> Researcher: [Points to hook.] What if you take that off?
> KN7: [Removes hook.] Oh yeah it's on zero . . .

Indeed even when the pupils did try to use scientific terminology to refer to observable objects (level ii) their lack of familiarity with these terms meant that these labels were sometimes applied incorrectly:

KN15: It takes [points to the 5 kilograms suspended from the Newton-meter] 500 kilometres *(sic)* to pull it down
KN16: That's 500 kilograms *(sic)*.
KN15: No kilometres *(sic)*.
KN14: [Points to the letters gm stamped on each mass.] g m, that's grams to gilometers *(sic)* . . .

It must be emphasized that, while Dr Starbeck was the only teacher observed to use a strategy to ensure that most of the pupils were fully familiar with the ideas that he intended them to use, his was not the only task in which pupils talked about the observables using relevant scientific ideas intended by the teacher as the following example shows:

Researcher: [Points to pupils' results] And what does that show you?
RL10: That it don't matter where you put the volt meter in parallel circuits it'll always have the same pressure on it as the voltage is the same.
Researcher What about series circuits?
RL10: That, that if you use the voltage to connect on one bulb it'll be half what it is taken off by the whole thing *(sic)* . . .

What I hope the example of Dr Starbeck's lesson illustrates is that practical tasks can be made more effective in terms of doing with ideas if the lesson time is divided more equitably between issues relating to doing with observables and doing with ideas. Certainly, in the case of the task used by Dr Starbeck, the time devoted to the development of the non-scientific model provided the opportunity for the pupils to familiarize themselves with the terms and ideas with which he wanted them to think about the task.

In essence how you divide up your lesson time will, of necessity, be a compromise. You want your pupils to *do* things so it makes sense that you need to devote time to procedural instructions. However, if you also want your pupils to *learn* then it is imperative that you devote a similar proportion of the lesson time to scaffolding and developing ideas. In this respect I would suggest, as we saw in the example drawn from Dr Starbeck's lesson, that shorter practical tasks embedded within a lesson that includes other non-practical elements offers the optimum means of maximizing the effectiveness of your practical task at levels 1 and 2 and across both domains.

In the following chapter I want to draw together all of the elements we have considered and in doing so suggest that practical work, while an essential feature of science education, can be made much more effective.

6 Conclusion

Chapter Outline

An overview of practical work

In order to provide an overview of practical work I want to start by suggesting that many teachers use practical work, despite the professional reasons that they might give, because they feel that doing so is an integral part of what it *means* to be 'a science teacher' (Donnelly, 1998). That is, part of the essence of being 'a science teacher' entails the use of practical work whenever possible in their teaching practice. This is not, of course, to claim that all science teachers who use practical work are necessarily *effective* teachers. From this perspective, claims made by teachers as to the effectiveness, and affective value, of practical work do not necessarily reflect firmly held personal beliefs, but represent what they believe to be appropriate professional responses that they provide when challenged to justify their use of practical work. Such a view shares a number of similarities to that made by McClelland (1984) who claims that this form of response 'may be said to be part of the professional armoury of those like teachers and politicians who may be faced with unexpected questions in circumstances where an admission of ignorance might be damaging' (p. 4). While I would suggest that 'ignorance' is too strong a word, it does appear that many teachers respond to questions about their professional practice in a way that they believe science teachers (qua science teacher) are expected to – and this might be country dependent – rather than necessarily what they might actually believe. This form of response has been referred to previously as 'role selection' (Anderson et al., 1975; Webb et al., 1966) and it is characterized by a respondent's 'selection of responses perceived as "proper" or expected in the situation'. (Anderson et al., 1975 p. 319). In this context I would suggest that the terms 'proper' or 'expected' can be seen as reflecting 'taken-for-granted traditions of practice, articulated with the explicitly more normative (though not necessarily more powerful) canons of "good practice"' (Donnelly, 1998 p. 594).

The fact that similar claims about the effectiveness, and affective value, of practical work have been made by teachers just completing their teacher training (Wellington 1998), as are made by experienced teachers suggests that these beliefs and/or claims are adopted, as part of a body of accepted professional wisdom, by many trainee teachers perhaps even prior to taking up their first teaching position during their initial teacher training. Indeed, it is highly probable that some of those teachers, who, for example, talk about the 'motivational' value of practical work, and/or its effectiveness in developing pupils' conceptual understanding, would, as initial teacher training mentors themselves, make similar claims when discussing the use of practical work with trainee teachers. Hodson (1996) has suggested that 'because experiments are widely used in science, intending science teachers become socialized, during their own science education, into regarding them as essential to science education' (p. 756). It is the adoption, and use, of these beliefs and/or claims that, I suggest, indicates a teacher's membership of what might usefully be described as the 'teaching community'.

That teachers make such claims in the belief that they reflect the accepted wisdom of the educational community helps to explain why many may feel justified in making them even though it is unlikely that they are aware of any specific educational research to support their beliefs. Indeed Ratcliffe et al. (2004) have found that despite the claims that teachers make,

> Few teachers gave examples of the influence of particular pieces of research, or research findings… More commonly research influences were referred to in *general* and *unspecified* terms… for example as supporting a teacher's preference for using practical work. (p. 72. Italics added)

Yet the findings reported by Wellington (1998) also show that some trainee teachers, when questioned about why they would use practical work, offer a more 'pragmatic' set of reasons. The claims made by these trainee teachers appear, from their similarity to the sorts of claims frequently made by pupils, to reflect their *personal,* as opposed to *professional,* beliefs about practical work based, arguably, on their own experiences as pupils. For example, some of the claims as to why practical work should be used included: "'to make a change from theory work"; "something else to do apart from lessons"; "keeps kids quiet"; "makes lessons more interesting"; "they break up lessons to keep the kids entertained"; "fun – sometimes!"; "nice change"' (Wellington, 1998 p. 6). Similar pragmatic responses were given by some of the more experienced teachers within this study, when they felt more relaxed, and less professionally challenged – for example, over a coffee in the staff-room, rather than in the laboratory during the lesson observation or when surrounded by colleagues. Many teachers appeared to operate a form of 'dualism' in which 'appropriate' professional responses were given when responding to questions in a profes-sional capacity, while another set of pragmatic responses, such as those listed above, were given when responding to questions in an informal capacity. This is not to suggest that any particular set of responses – professional or prag-matic – is, in some sense, a better representation of the 'truth' about what teach-ers actually believe than another, just that two distinctly different views are given. However, the issue of how and why practical work was used, as well as its effectiveness and affective value are, I suggest, easier to understand if we see the pragmatic, rather than the 'appropriate' professional, reasons as the primary influence on how teachers use practical work. If pragmatic reasons, such as those listed above in which practical work is essentially perceived as an enjoyable *alternative* to 'theory', are seen as influencing teachers' practice, then it helps to explain why teachers place the emphasis on doing with objects, materials and phenomena rather than learning about ideas or 'theory' in what is essentially seen as a *practical* lesson – by which I mean a lesson devoted primarily to 'hands-on' rather than cerebral activity.

This is not to say that science teachers do not *expect* pupils to learn as a result of getting them to successfully do with objects, materials and phenomena. That teachers' frequently include the learning of scientific ideas among their objectives for a practical lesson indicates, from the evident lack of planning as to *how* pupils will learn from doing and the fact that very little, if any, time was devoted to scaffolding the development of appropriate ideas, that many teachers still appear (consciously or unconsciously) to accept the validity of a 'discovery based' view of learning. These teachers consider themselves justified in expecting that the ideas that they intended the pupils to learn will 'emerge' from the phenomena and/or data of their own accord provided only that the pupils are able to produce them successfully (Solomon, 1994; Driver, 1983). And while the pupils *do* learn, by successfully producing the phenomena, what they learn about tends to be observable features of objects, materials and phenomena rather than about ideas. This is not to say that scientific knowledge cannot 'emerge' as a consequence of personal discovery but rather, as has been pointed out (Newman, 1982; Hirst and Peters, 1970), that,

> [The] natural home [for discovery based learning] would seem to be in contexts where the person is learning essentially on his own, where as a matter of fact there is no teacher, or where there could not possibly be a teacher, because what is to be learnt is as yet unknown… But, by contrast, the whole point of schooling is that there is a teacher whose function it is to bring about learning. (Hirst and Peters, 1970 p. 78)

Even if practical work were only *as effective as* alternative non-practical methods of teaching, in getting pupils to learn, I would suggest that, from a pragmatic perspective, its use still offers two distinct advantages over alternative, non-practical, 'theory' lessons. The first is that pupils claim to like it. While such claims are, generally speaking, little more than statements of relative preference, they still illustrate that even among those pupils who claim to dislike science and to have no intention of pursuing it post compulsion, practical work is the preferred method of being taught science. In this context practical work is perceived, both by pupils *and* teachers, as the 'carrot' to the 'stick' of theory. Given that many pupils, especially those of low academic ability, find the cognitively demanding 'theory' part of science much more difficult than simply 'doing' practical work, they often exhibit their frustration and/or displeasure, at having to do 'theory' in which they are far more likely to be seen to fail, through poor behaviour during the lesson.

If, as seems likely, teachers recognize that academically low ability pupils will find learning about scientific ideas difficult, *whatever* teaching tactic they use, then the fact that pupils prefer practical work, and are likely to be better behaved if allowed to do it, means that one important advantage of the use of practical work is that, in terms of classroom management, it makes the *teaching* of science easier despite the added issue of safety in the laboratory.

The second advantage that the use of 'recipe' style practical work, with its emphasis on 'doing' rather than 'learning', offers is that it reduces the need for extended discussion and explanation, that make greater demands on teachers' subject knowledge, making it a particularly attractive option among teachers teaching outside of their subject specialism. For these teachers the use of 'recipe' style tasks provides a way of ensuring that, even if they themselves are less than fully secure with the associated concepts, they are still able to ensure that the pupils, by adhering rigorously to the 'recipe' (often part of a departmental scheme of work), are able to do with and, from a 'discovery based' view of learning, learn about objects, materials and phenomena.

Among the set of 'appropriate' professional beliefs that teachers can give when questioned is that the use of practical work 'motivates' pupils towards science and/or that it generates personal interest in a subject or topic. Yet, in marked contrast to these 'appropriate' professional beliefs, the teachers' own personal, pragmatic, beliefs are that the affective value of practical work was essentially limited to providing short-term (i.e. non-enduring) situational interest, designed to keep pupils engaged during a specific lesson. Even allowing for the fact that some pupils might be prevented from pursuing science post compulsion, because of the selective nature of 'A' level choice in England, it appears difficult to reconcile the 'appropriate' professional claims, regarding the affective value of practical work, with the undeniable fact that a large number of pupils choose, despite having undertaken practical work regularly over a period of five years, not to pursue science post compulsion. The pragmatic view, I would suggest, is that practical work essentially provides a form of short-term engagement, which is viewed by pupils as the most enjoyable option within a compulsory subject that many of them would prefer not to be doing. From this perspective pupils' enjoyment of practical work arises because it provides opportunities to 'mess around' and talk to friends, and, as Bennett (2003) notes, this talk is not always about the science task at hand. Such a view helps to explain why many pupils claim both to enjoy practical work and yet are just as keen in their desire to drop science at the earliest possible opportunity. Indeed, I would tentatively suggest to you that rather than motivating pupils towards science per se doing practical work frequently generates little more than a desire to do ever more practical work as a means of avoiding the need to engage with scientific ideas at a meaningful, if sometimes difficult, conceptual level.

I think that it is the pragmatic claims rather than the professional ones that best account for how and why many teachers use practical work. Similarly, by distinguishing between the rhetoric and the reality of the claims relating to the affective value of practical work it may be possible to explain not only why teachers use it, but also why those pupils who claim to like it so much still persist in dropping science in large numbers at the end of Key Stage 4.

Understanding practical work

While some of the claims in this book are not in themselves surprising – the effectiveness of practical work as a means of teaching scientific knowledge has already been widely questioned (Gott and Duggan, 1996; Clackson and Wright, 1992; Hodson, 1990) – this book has, through the use of a relatively large number of case studies provided you with a considerable amount of evidence that might otherwise have been anecdotal. Furthermore, because of the fact that data saturation was achieved (the critical case of Dr Starbeck was highly unusual and I had to specifically seek out his participation in the study) I hope this book provides you with a much needed, rhetoric free, insight into the typical use of practical work in secondary school science.

The book has also highlighted the fact that there is little evidence to show that teachers frequently design, or use, practical tasks with the specific intention of developing conceptual understanding, or see the need to do so. Indeed it has shown that much practical work takes place within the framework of what appears to be a tacitly accepted 'discovery based' approach to teaching and learning, in which teachers appear to assume that pupils will 'discover' the relevant scientific ideas for themselves simply by generating and observing the appropriate phenomena and/or data. I hope that this book has also contributed to your understanding of the effectiveness of practical work in the affective domain. In this respect we have seen that despite the frequent and widespread claims regarding the motivational value of practical work, what teachers actually mean when they talk about 'motivation', and in fact what practical work has been shown to be effective in generating, is referred to, in psychological terminology, as short-term (non-enduring) situational interest. Moreover, I hope to have drawn your attention to the fact that, with the exception of some Year 7 pupils, many of the claims made by pupils to like practical work are, in fact, expressions of relative preference that do not necessarily indicate a liking of science per se or reflect a desire to pursue its study beyond Key Stage 4.

Implications for practice

Science education is, as Millar (1991) has suggested, 'irreducibly an interplay between experiment and theory, and so a total separation of theory and experiment is neither desirable nor possible' (p. 43). What I have argued throughout this book is that although teachers use both practical lessons and non–practical 'theory' lessons there is little, if any, evidence of an interplay between experiment and theory *within* the context of a practical lesson – the planned and deliberate construction of a bridge that would be necessary to link the domain of observables with the domain of ideas, required if effective learning is to occur. This is not to say that such a linkage might not be developed in lessons following the practical work, but rather that it does not frequently occur during the practical lessons themselves nor do many teachers, when questioned, state or imply that it will be developed in subsequent lessons.

Two principal implications for practice arise from this. Firstly there is a need for greater clarity among teachers about what pupils can realistically be expected to achieve, *both* in terms of 'doing' and 'learning', in practical lessons that seldom last more than 60 minutes and, with arrival and registration at the beginning of the lesson and the need to pack away at the end, are, in reality, unlikely to exceed 50 minutes. Secondly there is a need, as Millar (2004) has pointed out, for teachers to recognize that 'Ideas and explanations do not simply 'emerge' from data' (p. 3). If pupils are to *learn* from, rather than merely produce, phenomena, the 'discovery based' view of learning that is clearly evident in the way many teachers use practical work, despite its rejection by most philosophers of science (Millar 2004), needs to be replaced by a hypothetico-deductive view of learning in which teachers recognize that 'doing' with objects, materials and phenomena is unlikely to lead to the pupils 'learning' about scientific ideas and concepts unless they are also provided with what Wood et al. (1976) term a 'scaffold' (p. 90). The process of scaffolding provides the initial means by which pupils are helped to 'see' the phenomena in the same 'scientific way' that the teacher 'sees' it (Ogborn et al., 1996). Indeed, as Lunetta (1998) has argued, 'laboratory inquiry alone is not sufficient to enable students to construct the complex conceptual understandings of the contemporary scientific community. If students' understandings are to be changed towards those of accepted science, then intervention and negotiation with an authority, usually a teacher, is essential' (p. 252). The issue then is the form that this intervention and negotiation with the teacher takes and the extent to which the need for it is acknowledged and built into the practical task by the teacher.

An example of a strategy designed to get pupils thinking about a particular practical task, as opposed to merely 'doing' it in a mechanical, often unthinking, manner, is the Predict-Observe-Explain (POE) task structure designed by White and Gunstone (1992). In these (POE) tasks the pupils are required to predict, and write down, what they expect to observe *before* they carry out the task and then, having carried out the task, they have to explain what they observed, which might not necessarily be the same as what they predicted. Although this strategy was used in a number of the observed practical lessons there was little evidence to suggest that teachers (or pupils) saw it as anything other than something that had to be done at the start of a sequence of procedural instructions that were essentially designed to get the pupils to produce the desired phenomenon. In one case, when Mr Overton used this strategy, the pupils were required to predict, by writing either 'yes' or 'no' on a pre-printed table, whether a magnetic field would pass through a particular named material. As Mr Overton focused his introduction almost exclusively on what they were to do with objects, materials and phenomena the pupils appeared to see the unexplained *requirement*, that they make a prediction, as something that had to be done before they could move on to the 'real' part of the practical that involved 'doing' with objects and materials. Many of these pupils were observed rushing to complete the prediction table often inserting 'yes' and 'no' responses in what was subsequently found to be an unthinking and essentially random manner. This is not to say that the POE strategy cannot be effective, indeed both Millar (2004) and Lunetta (1998) have reported that it has been found to be 'strikingly successful' (Millar, 2004 p. 10). However, it suggests that if it is to be successful teachers must be helped to appreciate that the Predict-Explain components of the POE are as, if not more, important than the need to generate, and subsequently observe, the phenomena. Another strategy that might be incorporated into a wide range of practical work in order to encourage pupils to 'think', as well as merely to 'do', is that developed by Tiberghien (1996) to help in the introduction of ideas about energy transfer among secondary school pupils. This strategy involves presenting the pupils with a prototypical approach, referred to as the 'seed' of a model, for representing simple processes in energy terms and exemplifying its use in one specific example. The pupils are then presented with other examples of energy transfer (electric motors raising weights, weights turning dynamos and the like) and are helped to think about, and represent, these new energy transfer process using the same 'seed' model.

Given the perceived need for, and apparent success of, 'recipe' style tasks as a means of helping to get a large majority of pupils, irrespective of their academic ability, to do what the teacher intended with objects and/or phenomena in the limited time available, it would be both counter-productive, and unrealistic, to expect teachers to abandon their use in practical lessons. However, by recognizing the importance of developing a pupil's conceptual understanding of the phenomena, as well as merely getting them to produce them, teachers might be encouraged to divide the time available within practical lesson more equitably between 'doing' and 'learning'. This is not to say that 'doing' and 'learning' need to be rigidly separated, but that teachers should try to devote a greater proportion of the lesson time to helping the pupils to use the ideas associated with the phenomena that they have produced, rather than seeing the successful production of the phenomena as an end in itself. Clearly, given the time constraints under which teachers operate, devoting a greater proportion of time to 'learning' is achievable only if less time is devoted to 'doing'. Yet what was observed in the practical lesson taught by Dr Starbeck was that these two objectives are not mutually exclusive. Indeed, by using a closed, 'recipe' style, task to enable the pupils to quickly, and successfully, complete relatively *short* practical tasks, Dr Starbeck was able to devote an approximately equal amount of time to the development of a teaching model that served as a scaffold between the pupils' observations and the scientific ideas that he intended them to learn about.

One possible suggestion that might help in achieving this more equitable division of lesson time, between the domains of 'observables' and 'ideas', would be for teachers to make use of the 2 x 2 effectiveness matrix to audit the practical tasks they use. By suggesting that teachers fill in such a matrix for each task it would help them to consider and address the specific issue of what they intended pupils to 'do' and 'learn', not only in the domain of observables, but also in the domain of ideas. By breaking their objectives up into 'doing' and 'learning' in both domains, teachers may be better able to plan how to allocate time to each objective and, because the completed matrix provides evidence as to what would be required of the pupils *if* the practical lesson was to be effective, they can focus their attention on how best to achieve these aims. I therefore tentatively suggest, given the potential value that the use of such a matrix offers, that you might make use of it in your own science teaching.

In conclusion it must be recognized that although science deals with the natural world, practical work cannot (and should not) be used to make science into something it is not – a *solely* 'hands-on' activity. We use novel and exciting practical tasks to arouse pupils' interest in our subject from the moment they visit our secondary schools on Open Day in Year 6. However, if we are successful it is often as a result of having presented an image of science that, while exciting, fun and enjoyable, is arguably false and ultimately unsustainable. In effect what we have sold the pupils is not a science that involves meaningful cognitive engagement with difficult (although interesting) ideas, but a science that is quintessentially a simple, conceptually undemanding, 'hands-on' type activity that anyone can do, with little need for much thought, provided that they follow the 'recipe'. As long as the façade holds then we, and our subject, remain popular. However, we cannot put off indefinitely the need to teach the pupils about what are, relatively speaking, conceptually challenging scientific ideas and, as a consequence, it becomes ever more difficult to maintain the façade that we have created. Indeed it appears that the façade is, in many schools, already beginning to crumble from as early as the end of Year 7. Likewise because we use practical work to present a particular image of science, an image designed to appeal to pupils of all academic abilities, it should come as little surprise to us that pupils come to see practical work as being the 'nice', conceptually undemanding, part of science and arrive at science lessons hoping to do it. Indeed we, as teachers, help to create this image of practical work by removing anything that we perceive as being detrimental to the effective 'doing' of the practical task, such as the need to write which, for example, we minimize with the use of work sheets. We reduce or remove the need for independent thought, and the possibility that such thought presents for error, by using highly structured 'recipe' style tasks to ensure that all our pupils, irrespective of whether they think about the task or not, are able to produce the phenomenon that we want them to see. Many pupils like this because doing without thinking is an 'easy' option. What I hope to have shown you is that, for most teachers, the focus of their attention is devoted towards getting their pupils to 'do' with, and 'learn' about, objects, materials and phenomena rather than the cognitively more demanding 'doing' with, and 'learning' about, ideas relating to those phenomena. Furthermore, their use of a method of teaching that is preferred by the pupils, and is arguably no less effective in getting the pupils to learn about ideas than a method of teaching that they do not like, often makes the issue of class management easier. While there might be situations when health and safety considerations preclude allowing pupils who are behaviourally difficult to manage, and who have little interest in science, to undertake practical work, these will arguably constitute only a fraction of the practical tasks that could be used safely with such pupils.

I would like to end by suggesting that the overall effectiveness of practical work can be improved but that if this is to happen it is essential that science teachers appreciate, to a far greater extent than is currently the case, the role of practical work as a bridge between the two domains of knowledge. If this is to occur it will also require teachers to relinquish the 'discovery based' view of learning, in which 'doing' and 'learning' about ideas are seen to emerge of their own accord from the successful production of a phenomenon, and embrace a hypothetico-deductive approach in which practical work needs to be designed with the explicit aim of helping to 'scaffold' (Wood et al., 1976) pupils' efforts to form links between the domain of objects, materials and phenomena and the domain of ideas.

Whether, having read this book and thought about the issues, you agree or disagree with what I have written does not matter anywhere near as much as the fact that you have thought critically about the effectiveness and affective value of practical work and will, I believe, be a better teacher for having done so.

References

Abrahams, I. Z. (2005). 'Between rhetoric and reality: The use and effectiveness of practical work in secondary school science.' Unpublished PhD thesis. York: University of York.

Abrahams, I. Z. (2007a). 'Practical work: It's better than writing but does it motivate?' *Education in Science* 224, 10–11.

Abrahams, I. Z. (2007b). 'An unrealistic image of science.' *School Science Review* 88 (324), 119–22.

Abrahams, I. (2009). 'Does practical work really motivate? A study of the affective value of practical work in secondary school science.' *International Journal of Science Education.* 31 (17), 2335–53.

Abrahams, I. and Millar, R. (2008). 'Does practical work really work? A study of the effectiveness of practical work as a teaching and learning method in school science.' *International Journal of Science Education.* 30 (14), 1945–69.

Abrahams, I. and Saglam, M. (2010). 'A study of teachers' views on practical work in secondary schools in England and Wales.' *International Journal of Science Education.* 32 (6), 753–68.

Adey, P., Shayer, M. and Yates, C. (1989). *Thinking Science: The Curriculum Materials of the CASE Project.* London: Nelson.

Aiken, L. R. and Aiken, D. R. (1969). 'Recent research on attitude concerning science.' *Science Education,* 53, 295–305.

Alexander, P. A. (1997). 'Mapping the multidimensional nature of domain learning: The interplay of cognitive, motivational, and strategic forces.' In M. L. Maehr and P. R. Pintrich, (eds), *Advances in Motivation and Achievement* (pp. 213–50). Greenwich, CT: JAI Press.

Alexander, P. A., Jetton, T. L. and Kulikowich, J. M. (1995). 'Interrelationship of knowledge, interest, and recall: Assessing a model of domain learning.' *Journal of Educational Psychology,* 87, 559–75.

American Association for the Advancement of Science (AAAS) (1967). *Science a Process Approach (SAPA).* Washington DC: AAAS.

Ames, C. (1992). 'Classroom; goals, structures and student motivation.' *Journal of Educational Psychology,* 84 (3), 261–71.

Anderson, S. B., Ball, S., Murphy, R. T.and Associates (1975). *Encyclopedia of Educational Evaluation: Concepts and Techniques for Evaluating Education and Training Programs.* London: Jossey-Bass.

Arce, J. and Betancourt, R. (1997). 'Student-designed experiments in scientific lab instruction.' *Journal of College Science Teaching,* November, 114–18.

Armstrong, H. E. (1903). *The Teaching of Scientific Method and Other Papers on Education.* London: Macmillan and Co.

Arons, A. (1993). 'Guiding insight and inquiry in the introductory physics laboratory.' *The Physics Teacher*, 31, 278–82.

Ausubel, D. P. (1968). *Educational Psychology*. New York: Holt, Rinehart and Winston, Inc.

Bandura, A. (1986). *Social Foundations of Thought and Action: A Social Cognitive Theory*. Englewood Cliffs, NJ: Prentice-Hall.

Bates, G. R. (1978). 'The role of the laboratory in secondary school science programs.' In M. B. Rowe (ed.), *What Research Says to the Science Teacher* (pp. 55–82). Washington DC: National Science Teachers Association.

Beatty, J. W. (1980). 'School science, its organisation and practical work in the 11–13 Age Range.' Unpublished MSc dissertation. University of Oxford.

Beatty, J. W.and Woolnough, B. E. (1982). 'Practical work in 11–13 science: the context, type and aims of current practice.' *British Educational Research Journal*, 8, 23–30.

Bencze, J. L. (1996). 'Correlational studies in school science: Breaking the science-experiment-certainty connection.' *School Science Review*, 78 (282), 95–101.

Bennett, J. (2003). *Teaching and Learning Science: A Guide to Recent Research and its Applications*. London: Continuum.

Ben-Zvi, R., Hofstein, A., Samuel, D.and Kempa, R. F. (1976). 'The attitude of high school students to the use of filmed experiments in laboratory instruction.' *Journal of Chemical Education*, 53, 575–77.

Ben-Zvi, R., Hofstein, A., Samuel, D.and Kempa, R. F. (1977). 'Modes of instruction in high school chemistry.' *Journal of Research in Science Teaching*, 14, 433–39.

Bergin, D. A. (1999). 'Influences on classroom interest.' *Educational Psychologist*, 34 (2), 87–98.

Berry, A., Mulhall, P., Gunstone, R.and Loughran, J. (1999). 'Helping students learn from laboratory work.' *Australian Science Teachers' Journal*, 45 (1), 27–31.

Blosser, P. E. (1981). *A Critical Review of the Role of the Laboratory in Science Teaching*. Science Education Information report. Columbus, OH.: Centre for Science and Mathematics Education, Ohio State University.

Blumenfeld, P. C.and Meece, J. L. (1988). 'Task factors, teaching behavior, and students' involvement and use of learning strategies in science.' *Elementary School Journal*, 88, 235–50.

Boud, D. J., Dunn, J., Kennedy, T. and Thorley, R. (1980). 'The aims of science laboratory courses: A survey of students, graduates and practising scientists.' *European Journal of Science Education*, 2, 415–28.

Braund, M. (1999). 'Electric drama to improve understanding in science.' *School Science Review*, 81 (294), 35–41.

Brodin, G. (1978). 'The role of the laboratory in the education of industrial physicists and engineers.' In J. G. Jones and J. L. Lewis, (eds), *The Role of the Laboratory in Physics Education* (pp. 4–14). Birmingham: Goodman and Sons.

Brooks, J. G. and Brooks, M. G. (1993). *In Search of Understanding: The Case for Constructivist Classrooms*. Virginia, U.S.A.: Association for Supervision and Curriculum Development.

Brophy, J. (1983) 'Conceptualizing student motivation.' *Educational Psychologist*, 18 (3), 200–15.

Brown, S. and McIntyre, D. (1993). *Making Sense of Teaching*. Buckingham: Open University Press.

Bruner, J. S. (1961). 'The act of discovery.' *Harvard Educational Review*, 32, 21–32.

Bryant, R. J. and Marek, E. M. (1987). 'They like lab-centered science: The teachers in our workshops tell us so.' *The Science Teacher*, 54, 42–45.

Burron, B., James, M. L. and Ambrosio, A. L. (1993). 'The effects of cooperative learning in a physical science course for elementary/middle level preservice teachers.' *Journal of Research in Science Teaching*, 30, 697–707.

Cerini, B., Murray, I. and Reiss, M. (2003). *Student Review of the Science Curriculum. Major Findings*. London: Planet Science/Institute of Education University of London/Science Museum. Available online at: http://www.planet-science.com/sciteach/review (accessed 17 January 2010).

Chang, H.- P. and Lederman, N. G. (1994). 'The effects of levels of co-operation within physical science laboratory groups on physical science achievement.' *Journal of Research in Science Teaching*, 31, 167–81.

Clackson, S. G. and Wright, D. K. (1992). 'An appraisal of practical work in science education.' *School Science Review*, 74 (266), 39–42.

Connell, L. (1971). 'Demonstration and individual practical work in science teaching: A review of opinions.' *School Science Review*, 52, 692–702.

Conoley, C. and Hills, P. (1998). *Chemistry*. London: Collins Educational.

Dawe, S. (2003). *Practical Work: The Universal Panacea?* http://www.bishops.k12.nf.ca/rriche/ed6620/practical.html (accessed August 2009).

Delamont, S., Beynon, J. and Atkinson, P. (1988). 'In the beginning was the Bunsen: The foundations of secondary school science.' *Qualitative Studies in Education*, 1 (4), 315–28.

Denny, M. and Chennell (1986). 'Science practicals: What do pupils think?' *European Journal of Science Education*, 8, 325–36.

Department of Education and Science (The Dainton Report) (1968). *Enquiry into the Flow of Candidates in Science and Technology into Higher Education*. London: Her Majesty's Stationary Office.

Department of Education and Science Policy Statement (1985). *Science 5–16: A Statement of Policy*. London: Her Majesty's Stationary Office.

Doherty, J. and Dawe, J. (1988). 'The relationship between development maturity and attitude to school science.' *Educational Studies*, 11, 93–107.

Donne, J. (1624). *Devotions Upon emergent Occasions. (Meditations xvii)*. http:// www.poetry-online.org/donne_for_whom_the_bell_tolls.html (accessed August 2009).

Donnelly, J. F. (1998). 'The place of the laboratory in secondary science teaching.' *International Journal of Science Education*, 20 (5), 585–96.

Donnelly, J., Buchan, A., Jenkins, E., Laws, P., and Welford, G. (1996). *Investigations by Order. Policy, Curriculum and Science Teachers' Work under the Education Reform Act*. Nafferton, UK: Studies in Education Ltd.

Driver, R. (1975). 'The name of the game.' *School Science Review*, 56 (197), 800–805.

Driver, R. (1983). *The Pupil as Scientist?* Milton Keynes: Open University Press.

Driver, R., Guesne, E. and Tiberghien, A. (1985). 'Some features of children's ideas and their implications for teaching.' In R. Driver, E. Guesne and A. Tiberghien (eds), *Children's Ideas in Science* (pp. 193–201). Milton Keynes: Open University Press.

Driver, R., Squires, A., Rushworth, P. and Wood-Robinson, V. (1994). *Making Sense of Secondary Science: Research into Children's Ideas*. London: Routledge.

Duschl, R. A. and Gitomer, D. H. (1997). 'Strategies and challenges to changing the focus of assessment and instruction in science classrooms.' *Educational Assessment*, 4 (1), 37–73.

Edgeworth, R. L. and Edgeworth, M. (1811). *Essays on Practical Education*. Third edition. London: J. Johnson and Co.

Edwards, J. and Power, C. (1990). 'Role of laboratory work in a national junior secondary science project: Australian science education programme (ASSEP).' In E. Hegarty-Hazel (ed.), *The Student Laboratory and the Science Curriculum* (pp. 315–36). London: Routledge.

Fordham, A. (1980). 'Student intrinsic motivation, science teaching practices and student learning.' *Research in Science Education*, 10, 108–17.

Gagné, R. M. and White, R. T. (1978). 'Memory structures and learning outcomes.' *Review of Educational Research*, 48, 187–222.

Gangoli, S. G. and Gurumurthy, C. (1995). 'A study of the effectiveness of a guided open-ended approach to physics experiments.' *International Journal of Science Education*, 17 (2), 233–41.

Gardner, P. L. (1975). 'Attitudes to science.' *Studies in Science Education*, 2, 1–41.

Gardner, P. L. and Gauld, C. F. (1990). 'Labwork and students' attitudes.' In E. Hegarty-Hazel (ed.), *The Student Laboratory and the Science Curriculum* (pp. 132–56). London: Routledge.

Garner, R., Gillingham, M. G. and White, C. S. (1989). 'Effects of "seductive details" on macroprocessing and microprocessing in adults and children.' *Cognition and Instruction*, 6, 41–57.

Garrett, R. M. and Roberts, I. F. (1982). 'Demonstration verses small group practical work in science education.' *Studies in Science Education*, 9, 109–45.

Gauld, C. F. and Hukins, A. A. (1980). 'Scientific attitudes: A review.' *Studies in Science Education*, 7, 129–61.

Gott, R. and Duggan, S. (1995). *Investigative Work in the Science Curriculum*. Buckingham: Open University Press.

Gott, R. and Duggan, S. (1996). 'Practical work: Its role in the understanding of evidence in science.' *International Journal of Science Education*, 18 (7), 791–806.

Gunstone, R. F. (1991). 'Reconstructing theory from practical experience.' In B. E. Woolnough (ed.), *Practical Science* (pp. 67–77). Milton Keynes: Open University Press.

Gunstone, R. F. and Champange, A. (1990). 'Promoting conceptual change in the laboratory.' In E. Hegarty-Hazel (ed.), *The Student Laboratory and the Science Curriculum* (pp. 159–82). London: Routledge.

Gunstone, R. and Watts, M. (2000). 'Force and motion.' In R. Driver, E. Guesne and A. Tiberghien (eds), *Children's Ideas in Science* (pp. 85–104). Buckingham: Open University Press.

Gurumurthy, C. (1988). 'A comparative study of the effectiveness of guided discovery approach of doing physics experiments versus instructed performance approach at pre-university level.' PhD Thesis. India: Mysore University.

Hacking, I. (1983). *Representing and Intervening*. Cambridge: Cambridge University Press.

Hannon, M. (1994). 'The place of investigations in science education.' *Education in Science*, January, 33–44.

Hart, C., Mulhall, P., Berry, A., Loughran, J. and Gunstone, R. (2000). 'What is the purpose of this experiment? Or can students learn something from doing experiments?' *Journal of Research in Science Education*, 37 (5), 655–75

Harvard, N. (1996). 'Student attitudes to studying A-level sciences.' *Public Understanding of Science*, 5 (4), 321–30.

Head, J. (1982). 'What can psychology contribute to science education?' *School Science Review*, 63, 631–42.

Heaney, S. (1971). 'The effects of three teaching methods and the ability of young pupils to solve problems in biology: An experimental and quantitative investigation.' *Journal of Biological Education*, 5, 219–28.

Hendley, D., Stables, S. and Stables, A. (1996). 'Pupils' subject preferences at Key Stage 3 in South Wales.' *Educational Studies*, 22, 177–87.

Henry, N.W. (1975). 'Objectives for laboratory work.' In P. L. Gardner (ed.), *The Structure of Science Education* (pp. 61–75). Hawthorn, Victoria: Longman.

Hewson, M. and Hewson, P. (1983). 'Effect of instruction using student prior knowledge and conceptual change strategies on science learning.' *Journal of research in Science Teaching*, 20 (8), 731–43.

Hidi, S. (1990). 'Interest and its contribution as a mental resource for learning.' *Review of Educational Research*, 60, 549–71

Hidi, S. and Anderson, V. (1992). 'Situational interest and its impact on reading and expository writing.' In K. Renninger, S. Hidi and A. Krapp, (eds), *The Role of Interest in Learning and Development* (pp. 215–38). Hillsdale, NJ.: Lawrence Erlbaum Associates.

Hidi, S. and Berdorff, D. (1998). 'Situational interest and learning.' In L. Hoffmann, A. Krapp, K. Renninger and J. Baumert, (eds), *Interest and Learning: Proceedings of the Seeon Conference on Interest and Gender* (pp. 74–90). Kiel, Germany: IPN.

Hidi, S. and Harackiewicz, J. M. (2000). 'Motivating the academically unmotivated: A critical issue for the 21st century.' *Review of Educational Research*, 70 (2), 151–79.

Hill, B. W. (1976). 'Using college chemistry to influence creativity.' *Journal of Research in Science Teaching*, 13, 71–77.

Hirst, P. H. and Peters, R. S. (1970). *The Logic of Education*. London: Routledge and Kegan Paul.

Hodson, D. (1989). *Children's Understanding of Science*. University of Auckland Science and Technology Education Centre. Occasional Publications.

Hodson, D. (1990). 'A critical look at practical work in school science.' *School Science Review*, 70 (256), 33–40.

Hodson, D. (1991). 'Practical work in science: Time for a reappraisal.' *Studies in Science Education*, 19, 175–84.

Hodson, D. (1992). 'Redefining and reorientating practical work in school science.' *School Science Review*, 73 (264), 65–78.

Hodson, D. (1996). 'Practical work in school science: Exploring some directions for change.' *International Journal of Science Education*, 18 (7), 755–60.

Hoffmann, L. and Häussler, P. (1998). 'An intervention project promoting girls' and boys' interest in physics.' In L. Hoffmann, A. Krapp, K. Renninger and J. Baumert, (eds), *Interest and Learning: Proceedings of the Seeon Conference on Interest and Gender* (pp. 301–16). Kiel, Germany: IPN.

Hofstein, A. (1988). 'Practical work and science education II.' In P. Fensham (ed.), *Development and Dilemmas in Science Education* (pp. 189–217). Lewes: The Falmer Press.

Hofstein, A., Ben-Zvi, R. and Samuel, D. (1976). 'The measurement of interest in, and attitude to laboratory work amongst Israeli high school students.' *Science Education*, 60, 401–11.

Hofstein, A. and Lunetta, V. N. (1982). 'The role of the laboratory in science teaching: Neglected aspects of research.' *Review of Educational Research*, 52, 201–18.

House of Commons Science and Technology Committee (2002). *Minutes of Evidence*. http://www. rsc. org/pdf/education/sciend1419.pdf (accessed August 2009).

Iran-Nejad, A. (1987). 'Cognitive and affective causes of interest and liking.' *Journal of Educational Psychology*, 79, 120–30.

Jackman, L. E. and Moellenberg, W. P. (1987). 'Evaluation of three instructional methods for teaching general chemistry.' *Journal of Chemical Education*, 64, 794–96.

Jakeways, R. (1986). 'Assessment of A-level physics (Nuffield) investigations.' *Physics Education*, 21, 212–14.

Jenkins, E. W. (1994). 'Public understanding of science and science education for action.' *Journal of Curriculum Studies*, 26, 601–12.

Johnson, S. (1987). 'Gender differences in science: Parallels in interest, experience and performance.' *International Journal of Science Education*, 9, 467–81.

Johnstone, A. H. (1980). 'Chemical education research: Facts, findings, and consequences.' *Chemistry Society Review*. 9 (3), 365–80.

Johnstone, A. H. and Kellett, N.C. (1980). 'Learning difficulties in school science: towards a working hypothesis.' *European Journal of Science Education*. 2, 175.

Johnstone, A. H. and Wham, A. J. B. (1982). 'The demands of practical work.'
Education in Chemistry, 19, 71–73.

Kelly, A. (1986). 'The development of children's attitudes to science.' *European Journal of Science Education*, 8 (4), 399–412.

Kempa, R. F. and Palmer, C. R. (1974). 'The effectiveness of video-tape recorded demonstration in the learning of manipulative skills in practical chemistry.' *Journal of Educational Technology*, 5 (1), 62–71.

Kerr, J. F. (1964). *Practical Work in School Science*. Leicester: Leicester University Press.

Kirschner, P. (1992). 'Epistemology, practical work and academic skills in science education.' *Science Education*, 1, 273–99.

Krapp, A., Hidi, S. and Renninger, K. A. (1992). 'Interest, learning, and development.' In K.A. Renninger, S. Hidi and A. Krapp (eds), *The Role of Interest in Learning and Development* (pp. 3–25). Hillsdale, NJ.: Lawrence Erlbaum Associates.

Kreitler, H. and Kreitler, S. (1974). 'The role of experiment in science education.' *Instructional Science*, 3, 75–88.

Kruglak, H. and Wall, C. N. (1959). *Laboratory Performance Tests for general physics*. For the National Science Foundation; Western Michigan University, Kalamazoo, Michigan.

Langeveld, M. J. (1965). 'In search of research.' In *Paedagogica Europoea: The European Year Book of Educational Research* 1. Amsterdam: Elsevier.

Layton, D. (1990). 'Student laboratory practice and the history and philosophy if science.' In E. Hegarty-Hazel (ed.), *The Student Laboratory and the Science Curriculum* (pp. 37–59). London: Routledge.

Lazarowitz, R. and Tamir, P. (1994). 'Research on using laboratory instruction in science.' In D. L. Gabel (ed.), *Handbook of Research on Science Teaching and Learning* (pp. 94–130). New York: Macmillan.

Leach, J. and Scott, P. (1995). 'The demands of learning science concepts: Issues of theory and practice.' *School Science Review*, 76 (277), 47–52.

Lunetta, V. N. (1998). 'The school science laboratory: Historical perspectives and contexts for contemporary teaching.' In K. Tobin and B. Fraser (eds.), *International Handbook of Science Education*. Part 1, (pp. 249–62). Dordrecht: Kluwer.

Martin, M. (1979). 'Connections between philosophy of science and science education.' *Studies in Philosophy and Education,* 9 (4), 329–32.

Masters, R. and Nott, M. (1998). 'Implicit knowledge and science practical work in schools.' In J. Wellington (ed.), *Practical Work in School Science: Which Way Now?* (pp. 206–11). London: Routledge.

Matthews, M. R. and Winchester, I. (1989). 'History, science and science teaching.' *Interchange, 20,* 1–15.

Maxwell, G. (1962). 'The ontological status of theoretical entities.' *Minnesota Studies in the Philosophy of Science,* 3, 3–14.

McClelland, J. A. G. (1984). 'Alternative frameworks: Interpretation of evidence.' *European Journal of Science Education,* 6 (1), 1–6.

Middleton, J. A. (1995). 'A study of intrinsic motivation in the mathematics classroom: A personal constructs approach.' *Journal for Research in Mathematics Education,* 26, 254–79.

Millar, R. (1987a). *Teaching Physics as a Non-specialist: A Survey of the Views of Teachers Without Formal Physics Qualifications on Physics Teaching and INSET Provision.* York: Department of Education University of York.

Millar, R. (1987b). 'Towards a role for experiment in the science teaching laboratory.' *Studies in Science Education,* 14, 109–18.

Millar, R. (1989a). 'What is "scientific method" and can it be taught?' In J. Wellington (ed.), *Skills and Processes in Science Education* (pp. 47–61). London: Routledge.

Millar, R. (1989b). 'Constructive criticism.' *International Journal of Science Education,* 11 (5), 587–96.

Millar, R. (1991). 'A means to an end: The role of process in science education.' In B. E. Woolnough (ed.), *Practical Science* (pp. 43–52). Milton Keynes: Open University Press.

Millar, R. (1998). 'Rhetoric and reality: What practical work in science education is *really* for.' In J. Wellington. (ed.), *Practical Work in School Science: Which Way Now?* (pp. 16–31). London: Routledge.

Millar, R. (2002). 'Thinking about practical work.' In S. Amos and R. Booka, (eds), *Aspects of Teaching Secondary Science: Perspectives on Practice* (pp. 53–59). London: Routledge Falmer.

Millar, R. (2004). 'The role of practical work in the teaching and learning of science.' Paper prepared for the meeting: High school science laboratories: Role and vision. Washington DC: National Academy of Sciences.

Millar, R. and Driver, R. (1987). 'Beyond processes.' *Studies in Science Education,* 14, 33–62.

Millar, R., Le Maréchal, J-F. and Tiberghien, A. (1999). '"Mapping" the domain: Varieties of practical work.' In J. Leach and A. Paulsen (eds), *Practical Work in Science Education* (pp. 33–59). Dordrecht: Kluwer.

Millar, R. and Osborne, J. (eds). (1998). *Beyond 2000: Science Education for the Future.* London: King's College.

Mitchell, M. (1993). 'Situational interest: Its multifaceted structure in the secondary school mathematics classroom.' *Journal of Educational Psychology,* 85, 424–36.

Moreira, M. A. (1980). 'A non-traditional approach to the evaluation of laboratory in general physics courses.' *European Journal of Science Education,* 2, 441–48.

Mulopo, M. M. and Fowler, H. S. (1987). 'Effects of traditional and discovery instructional approaches on learning outcomes for learners of different intellectual development: A study of chemistry students in Zambia.' *Journal of Research in Science Teaching,* 24 (3), 217–27.

Murphy, P. K. and Alexander, P. (2000). 'A motivated exploration of motivation terminology. Quoted in S. Hidi and J. M. Harackiewicz, 'Motivating the academically unmotivated: A critical issue for the 21st century.' *Review of Educational Research*, 70 (2), 151–79.

National Curriculum Council, (1989). *Science in the National Curriculum: Non-statutory Guidance*. Section C16, 9.3. York: National Curriculum Council.

Newbury, N. F. (1934). *The Teaching of Chemistry*, London: Heinemann

Newman, D. (1982). 'Perspective-taking versus content in understanding lies.' Quarterly Newsletter of the laboratory of Comparative Human Cognition, 4, 26–29. Cited in B. Rogoff (1991). 'The joint socialisation of development by young children and adults.' In P. Light, S. Sheldon and M. Woodhead (eds), *Learning to Think* (pp. 26–29). London: Routledge.

Nott, M. and Wellington, J. (1997). 'Producing the evidence: Science teachers' initiations into practical work.' *Research in Science Education*, 27 (3), 395–409.

Nussbaum, J. (2000). 'The particulate nature of matter in the gaseous phase.' In R. Driver, E. Guesne and A. Tiberghien (eds), *Children's Ideas in Science* (pp. 124–44). Buckingham: Open University Press.

Ogborn, J., Kress, G., Martins, I. and McGillicuddy, K. (1996). *Explaining Science in the Classroom*. Buckingham: Open University Press.

Osborne, J. (1998). 'Science education without a laboratory?' In J. J. Wellington (ed.), *Practical Work in School Science: Which Way Now?* (pp. 156–73). London: Routledge.

Osborne, J. and Collins, S. (2001). 'Pupils' views of the role and value of the science curriculum: A focus-group study.' *International Journal of Science Education*, 23 (5), 441–67.

Osborne, J. F., Driver, R., Simon, S. and Collins, S. (1998). 'Attitudes to science: Issues and concerns.' *School Science Review*, 79 (288), 27–34.

Osborne, J., Simon, S. and Collins, S. (2003). 'Attitudes towards science: A review of the literature and its implications.' *International Journal of Science Education*, 25 (9), 1049–79.

Osborne, R. J. (1976). 'Using student attitudes to modify instruction in physics.' *Journal of Research in Science Teaching*, 13, 525–31.

Pell, T. and Jarvis, T. (2001). 'Developing attitude to science scales for use with children of ages from five to eleven years.' *International Journal of Science Education*, 23, 847–62.

Pickering, M. (1987). 'Laboratory education as a problem in organization.' *Journal of College Science Teaching*, 16, 187–89.

Popper, K. (1989). *Conjectures and Refutations: The Growth of Scientific Knowledge*. London: Routledge.

Prenzel, M. (1992). 'The selective persistence of interest.' In K. A. Renninger, S. Hidi and A. Krapp, (eds), *The Role of Interest in Learning and Development* (pp. 71–98). Hillsdale, NJ.: Lawrence Erlbaum Associates.

Ratcliffe, M., Bartholomews, H., Hames, V., Hind, A., Leach, J., Millar, R. and Osborne, J. (2004). *Science Education Practitioners' Views of Research and its Influence on Practice*. York: University of York.

Renninger, K. A. (1998). 'The roles of individual interest(s) and gender in learning: An overview of research on preschool and elementary school-aged children/students.' In L. Hoffmann, A. Krapp, K. Renninger and J. Baumert (eds), *Interest and Learning: Proceedings of the Seeon Conference on Interest and Gender* (pp. 165–75). Kiel, Germany: IPN.

Report of Science Masters' Association, (1953). *Secondary Modern Science Teaching*. London: John Murray.

Report of Secondary School Examinations Council (Norwood Report) (1943). *Curriculum and Examinations in Secondary Schools.* London: Her Majesty's Stationary Office.

Richmond, P. E. (1978). 'Who needs laboratories?' In J. G. Jones and J. L. Lewis (eds), *The Role of the Laboratory in Physics Education* (pp. 349–50). Birmingham: Goodman and Sons.

Schiefele, U. (1991). 'Interest, learning and motivation.' *Educational Psychologist,* 26, 299–323.

Schiefele, U. (1996). 'Topic interest, text representation, and quality of experience.' *Contemporary Educational Psychology,* 12, 3–18.

Schiefele, U. (1998). 'Individual interest and learning, what we know and what we don't know.' In L. Hoffmann, A. Krapp, K. Renninger and J. Baumert (eds), *Interest and Learning: Proceedings of the Seeon Conference on Interest and Gender.* Kiel, Germany: IPN, pp. 91–104.

Schiefele, U., Krapp, A. and Winteler, A. (1992). 'Interest as a predictor of academic achivement: A meta analysis of research.' In K. A. Renninger, S. Hidi and A. Krapp (eds), *The Role of Interest in Learning and Development* (pp. 183–212). Hillsdale, NJ.: Erlbaum.

Screen, P. (1986). *Warwick Process Science.* Southampton: Ashford Press.

Selemes, C., Ashton, B. G., Meredith, H. M. and Newal, A. (1969). 'Attitudes to science and scientists.' *School Science Review,* 51, 7–22.

Shipstone, D. (2000). 'Electricity in simple circuits.' In R. Driver, E. Guesne and A. Tiberghien (eds), *Children's Ideas in Science* (pp. 33–51). Buckingham: Open University Press.

Shulman, L. D. and Tamir, P. (1973). 'Research on teaching in the natural sciences.' In R. M. W. Travers (ed.), *Second Handbook of Research on Teaching* (pp. 1098–148). Chicago: Rand McNally and Co.

Simon, S. (2000). 'Student's attitudes towards science.' In M. Monk and J. Osborne (eds), *Good Practice in Science Teaching: What Research Has to Say* (pp. 104–20). Buckingham: Open University Press.

Smith, V. (2002). 'Cutting off magnetism.' *The Heinemann science scheme:* Activity sheet J2c Core p. 253.

Solomon, J. (1999). 'Envisionment in practical work. Helping pupils to imagine concepts while carrying out experiments.' In J. Leach and A. Paulsen (eds), *Practical Work in Science Education—Recent Research Studies* (pp. 60–74). Roskilde/Dordrecht, The Netherlands: Roskilde University Press/ Kluwer.

Solomon, J. (1994). 'The laboratory comes of age.' In R. Levinson (ed.). *Teaching Science* (pp. 7–21). London: Routledge.

Solomon, J. (1988). 'Learning through experiment.' *Studies in Science Education,* 15, 103–08.

Stavy, R. and Tirosh, D. (1996). 'Intuitive rules in science and mathematic: The case of "more of A – more of B".' *International Journal of Science Education,* 18 (6), 653–67.

Swain, J., Monk, M. and Johnson, S. (1999). 'A comparative study of attitudes to the aims of practical work in science education in Egypt, Korea and the UK.' *International Journal of Science Education,* 21 (12), 1311–23.

Tamir, P. (1991). 'Practical work in school science: An analysis of current practice.' In B. E. Woolnough (ed.), *Practical Science* (pp. 13–20). Milton Keynes: Open University Press.

Tasker, R. (1981). 'Children's views and classroom experiences.' *Australian Science Teachers Journal,* 27, 33–37.

The Thomson Report, (1918). *Natural Science in Education.* Report of the committee on the position of natural science in the educational system of Great Britain. Her Majesty's Stationary Office.

Thijs, G. and Bosch, G. (1995). 'Cognitive effects of science experiments focusing on students' perceptions of force: A comparison of demonstrations and small group practicals.' *International Journal of Science Education*, 17 (3), 311–23.

Thompson, J. J. (ed.). (1975). *Practical Work in Sixth Form Science*. Oxford: Department of Educational Studies, University of Oxford.

Tiberghien, A. (1996). 'Construction of prototypical situations in teaching the concept of energy.' In G. Welford, J. Osborne and P. Scott (eds), *Research in Science Education in Europe. Current Issues and Themes* (pp. 100–14). London: Falmer Press.

Tiberghien, A. (2000). 'Designing teaching situations in the secondary school.' In R. Millar, J. Leach and J. Osborne (eds), *Improving Science Education: The Contribution of Research* (pp. 27–47). Buckingham: Open University Press.

Third International Mathematics and Science Study (TIMSS) (1999). International Science Report. isc. bc.edu/timss 1999. html (accessed May 2009).

Tobin, K. (1990). 'Research on science laboratory activities: In pursuit of better questions and answers to improve learning.' *School Science and Mathematics*, 90 (5), 403–18.

Van den Berg, E. and Giddings, G. (1992). *Laboratory Practical Work: An Alternative View of Laboratory Teaching*. Monograph. Western Australia: Curtin University, Science and Mathematics Education Centre.

Wade, S. E. and Adams, B. (1990). 'Effects of importance and interest on recall of biographical text.' *A Journal of Literacy*, 22, 331–53.

Wallace, G. (1996). 'Engaging with learning.' In J. Rudduck (ed.), *School Improvement: What Can Pupils Tell Us?* (pp. 56–69). London: David Fulton.

Ward, J. N. (1956). 'Group-study verses lecture-demonstration method in physical science instruction for general education college students.' *Journal of Experimental Education*, 24, 197–210.

Watson, F. G. (1963). 'Research on teaching science.' In N. L. Gage (ed.), *Handbook of Research on Teaching* (pp. 1031–59). Chicago: Rand McNally and Co.

Watson, J. R., Prieto, T. and Dillon, J. (1995). 'The effect of practical work on students' understanding of combustion.' *Journal of Research in Science Teaching*, 32 (5), 487–502.

Watson, R. and Fairbrother, R. (1993). 'Open ended work in science (OPENS) project: Managing investigations in the laboratory.' *School Science Review*, 75 (271), 31–38.

Webb, E.J., Campbell, D.T., Schwartz, R.D. and Sechrest, L. (1966). *Unobtrusive Measures: Nonreactive Research in the Social Sciences*. Chicago: Rand McNally.

Wellington, J. (1989). 'Skills and processes in science education: An introduction.' In J. Wellington (ed.), *Skills and Processes in Science Education* (pp. 5–20). London: Routledge.

Wellington, J. (1998). 'Practical work in science.' In J. Wellington (ed.), *Practical Work in School Science: Which Way Now?* (pp. 3–15). London: Routledge.

White, R. T. (1979). 'Relevance of practical work to comprehension of physics.' *Physics Education*, 14, 384–87.

White, R. T. (1988). *Learning Science*. Oxford: Blackwell.

White, R. T. (1991). 'Episodes and the purpose and conduct of practical work.' In Woolnough, B. E. (ed.), *Practical Science* (pp. 78–86). Milton Keynes: Open University Press.

White, R. T. (1996). 'The link between the laboratory and learning.' *International Journal of Science Education*, 18 (7), 761–74.

White, R. T. and Gunstone, R. (1992). *Probing Understanding*. London: Falmer Press.

Whitefield, R. C. (1980). 'Educational research and science teaching.' *School Science Review*, 60, 411–30.

Wickman, P. O. and Östman, L. (2001). 'University students during practical work: Can we make the learning process intelligible?' In H, Behrendt, R. Duit, W. Gräber, M Komorek, A. Kross and P. Reiska (eds), *Research in Science Education – Past, Present, and Future* (pp. 319–24). Dordrecht: Kluwer.

Wilkinson, J. and Ward, M. (1997). 'A comparative study of students' and their teacher's perceptions of laboratory work in secondary schools.' *Research in Science Education*, 27 (4), 599–610.

Windschitl, M. and Andre, T. (1998). 'Using computer simulation to enhance conceptual change: The roles of constructivist instruction and student epistemological beliefs.' *Journal of Research in Science Teaching*, 35 (2), 144–60.

Wood, D., Bruner, J. S. and Ross, G. (1976). 'The role of tutoring in problem solving.' *Journal of Child Psychology and Psychiatry*, 17, 89–100.

Woolnough B. E. and Allsop T. (1985). *Practical Work in Science*, Cambridge: Cambridge University Press.

Yager, R., Engen, H. and Snider, B. (1969). 'Effects of the laboratory and demonstration methods upon the outcomes of instruction in secondary biology.' *Journal of Research in Science Teaching*, 6, 76–86.

Index